RISE

of the

Good woman

Published by
Mynd Matters Publishing
715 Peachtree Street NE,
Suites 100 & 200, Atlanta, GA 30308

978-1-953307-29-3 (Pbk)
978-1-953307-30-9 (eBook)

FIRST EDITION

RISE

of the
Good
woman

A 22-DAY GUIDE TO BECOMING A BETTER YOU

STACY LLOYD

To my Father, Raymond E. Lloyd Jr.,
for always trying to mold me into a good girl. As the words to this
book formed sentences, it all came together. I appreciate the tough
love and effort to save me from myself. You are a great earthly
father and I am truly proud to be your daughter. I pray those who
read this book feel the blessings of being good. The same way I am
to have a dad like you.

CONTENTS

"Your granny's 40-50+ year marriage isn't goals to me if she had to accept non-stop infidelities, struggle love, 2nd class citizenship in her home, silencing herself to survive it, seeing her man's face in neighborhood kids, and her worth only being based off her culinary and child-rearing abilities. These are not goals."

-Lateisha Dionne

INTRODUCTION

When I turned thirty-eight, I knew I wanted my life to be different from previous years. I decided to take my own advice and write a year's worth of goals. I segmented it into categories including, finance and career, generosity, family and friends, health and fitness, travel, and a bucket list of miscellaneous goals that didn't neatly fit into any particular category.

It was when I got to the spiritual section that my list of dreams for the year seemed a bit impossible. Goals such as, "Get married! Fall in love first, ha!" (Yes, I made it a goal to get married in a year) were initially an exciting fantasy and yes, perhaps impossible. But with God all things are possible, right? So, I decided not to revise or remove it.

SPIRITUAL-->
GOAL: Get married! Fall in love first, ha!
☑ 1. Making sure I've forgiven all past relationships
☑ 2. Clear all energy for husband, leave old in the past
☑ 3. Make room for husband in all areas, focus and praise God in advance for husband
☑ 4. Learn as much as you can about being a good wife (Bible, Proverbs 31), cooking, getting in the mindset of considering another. Think marriage not singleness
☑ 5.Become more feminine

GOAL: Be a better me spiritually
☑ 1. Better Prayer life. Keep God 1st.
☑ 2. Know the word. Study to show myself approved.
☑ 3. Share what learn, spread the word and love. Lots of love
☑ 4. Be fearless + bold. Just do it
☑ 5. Don't wait. Don't procrastinate. MOVE.

I would go on to make another list of actionable steps to achieve this particular goal. For the marriage one, step four was the biggie. I cook but the goal was to add variety to keep things fresh. I can be selfish at times so I could use some work in that area. Where do I start? How does one prepare for marriage? Can you prepare for marriage? All I knew was the Proverbs 31 passage. I read it more times than I could count. I figured I would not have a problem doing "my part" to prepare. However, it wasn't as easy as I thought it would be. You see, I come from a family tree riddled with divorce. Out of my parents and their siblings, eleven couples total, only one was in their original marriage. And unfortunately, my aunt's husband had just died. I had a few examples outside of my family but not much during my impressionable years as a child. My dad's parents seemed to work well together but their displays of affection lacked. My mother's folks are still alive and married but their love really lacks affection too and they fuss incessantly. They have that annoying, nagging "I-love-you-but-we-fuss-all-the-time-but-I'm-not-going-to-divorce-you-because-I-can't-live-without-you" kind of love. They love each other so much they get on each other's last nerve. It's funny and rather odd.

In my formative years, I saw a lot of dysfunction. Because it was ordained by God and as a Christian, I assumed what I was witnessing was love and correct, I thought it wasn't my role to question it. I grew up wanting to get married yet afraid of the outcome. I feared it would fail and end up in divorce like the majority of my family. So, at the ripe age of thirty-eight, I had to make a change. In addition to learning as much as I could about how to be a good wife and woman, I had to shift my perception of love and marriage.

* * *

Where is the real, almost fantasy, love? That Cliff and Claire Huxtable, television love. Does it exist? Let's be clear, I'm not one of those princess fantasy little girls turned grown woman. I just want the kind of love that exists when you look at your partner in disbelief at how blessed you are to have one another. Not, "It's cheaper to keep her, I'll just tolerate her" kind of love. Definitely not the "It is better to marry than burn so we get married so we don't burn because we think we love each other" love. And lastly the, "I am about to turn eighteen and I have to leave the house so I marry the first cute thang with a wide smile" love. No, you can have that love.

> "People may fail me for whatever reason but my Higher Power never does. With my relationship with my Higher Power, I feel loved, I feel safe, I feel free."
> **JADA PINKETT SMITH**

What is love? What does it mean to me and how do I show it? Getting a handle on how to rid myself of the not-too-pleasant view of love was where I had to start. I actually discovered my childhood played a major role and I'd developed both mommy and daddy issues. While I was aware of the daddy issues, the mommy part threw me for a loop. As God would have it, that therapeutic healing came in the form of a book, a diary, to my younger self. I was able to address my issues and forgive and ask God to help heal my wounded heart. It freed me to truly love myself. To be in acceptance of the total essence of Stacy. Self-love is a beautiful thing. It is essential. It is where each individual should start. God rescued me. The validation from my folks was no longer a necessity and I could walk in freedom.

Once the foundation of self-love and true acceptance was evident, I worked on past relationships. I really thought I'd done the work here, too.

My former boyfriend (my young guy), K, and I were starting to move in different directions. We didn't talk about it but I knew it in my heart. A move from Los Angeles to Atlanta at the end of 2014 was our gentle break-up. He is a really good guy and he'll make someone happy one day, but I knew it wasn't going to be me. The damage from that relationship was almost nonexistent. Our shared love was as precious as a forehead kiss. I learned a ton about upholding a man, keeping him encouraged, being soft and present. I learned how to talk and discuss things logically and with balance. To take the emotion and ego out of it. We argued less than a handful of times in three years. It was a stress-free relationship and I grew a ton. Most importantly, learning to be cognizant of what I said and how it landed on another person's ears was invaluable and for that, I remain grateful.

> "Self-love, a person's essential being that distinguishes them from others, especially considered as the object of introspection or reflexive action. An intense feeling of deep affection."
> -TAI SAWYER

From dedicating half of my thirties to him through our relationship to being okay with the thought of him with someone else, our connection spanned six years. At first, it's unimaginable to think of someone you were building a future with loving another person. But over time, feelings fade and what settled in that space was happiness and peace. I let go of what could have been and moved forward.

What I discovered towards the end of our relationship was the lack of self-love. It then became evident in all of my past relationships especially the one I had in college. I experienced verbal and emotional abuse and it stripped me down to the core. By the time I was in my thirties and dating K, I believed I'd done the work to rebuild. It turns out, I had not and realized I could not determine what I wanted to love if I had yet to love myself. I didn't know or love myself fully so how could I expect someone else to love me? How could I give love when I was unsure of the definition of the word? K was likely trying to love me but I existed as a shell of my own being. It wasn't until I spent adequate time alone after our breakup that God showed me, me. It was a master's course taught by The Master. I learned how to love and now I am open to my life's purpose partner.

I look forward to that part of my life and that is where this lovely book comes into play.

> "How do you find self-love? You dig. You isolate and you ache from being lonely. You heal. You accept, you look in the mirror and see God."
>
> -NIKKI WALTON

This master course became a quest to prepare. To seek out the answers, to learn as much as I could from various sources around me and utilize resources at my disposal and within reach. I read books like *The Wait* by Devon Franklin & Meagan Good; *Man Leads…Woman Follows, Everyone Wins* by Ro Elori Cutno; *Finding Mr. Forever* by Leslie Neland; *The 5 Love Languages: The Secret to Love That Lasts* by Gary Chapman; *Black Girl's Guide to Being Blissfully Feminine* by Candice Adewole and Proverbs 31: 10-31. It was nine months of intensive marriage prep. As I read, I also wrote books, one of which was clearing out the way for all of the other stuff I was rapidly learning. Self-love was the overall theme as well as having boundaries, standards, and allowing the man to be "the man." In addition to the books and Bible, I talked to those happily married men in reference to women, mothers, friends, and family. I also participated in two group fasts, praying specifically for my future husband. And then I joined a few Facebook groups, one of them being *Blissfully Feminine*. It was, shall I say, a lot. I believe God is going to present me to my future husband when the time is right and I don't want to slow down the process by not doing what I can on my end. I did and continue to do the work as a display of my faith.

> "As a woman, it's your responsibility to work on developing the fullness of who God created you to be before you give yourself to your husband."
>
> -DEVON FRANKLIN

Now, there is no perfect time to marry. No perfect time but God's perfect timing. I do believe God gives us choices as to whom we marry. Quite frankly, I could have been married by now if I was solely interested in the companionship of it. But I chose not to go that route at the time. I have since learned that marriage is every bit about walking in purpose together as it is sharing and enjoying life with one another. The more you know about yourself and your God-given purpose, the easier it is to make a choice about a romantic partnership. There are a lot of ways you can be compatible with someone but at the end of the day, what are you doing to help humanity? The bigger picture of marriage is kingdom building. In essence, leaving the world better than before you graced it.

> "Understand who you are as union, but also understand who you are independent of the union."
> -DEVON FRANKLIN

You're probably wondering how walking in the fullness of how God created you to be works. Well, throughout these pages, I provide insight and guidance. My intent is to help you tap into not only what God destined for your life, but how to be a good woman—a good human being. I'm on a crusade to raise the standard that has dropped when it comes to good versus evil, God's principles versus the world. This is a campaign for good women to take a stand and create a foundation of goodness across the globe.

You may be asking, but how do we take on such a task? I believe the Bible is the blueprint, the guide, the map, and the compass to keep our lives moving in the right direction. There are so many symbols, allegories, myths, and parables in the good book and reading it is like cracking a code. However, it is up to us to open it, read, study and interrupt what God is trying to convey to us pertaining to our lives. The only way to change things for the better is with God and His word. It's that simple. With God ALL things are possible.

Where do we begin, you ask? We start with God's intention for women described very well in Proverbs 31:10-31. It was in my discovery to prepare to be a wife that I realized how far off we are as women. We have really let the ball drop and allowed a lower standard of morality, role confusion, and too much compromise in our lifestyles.

Now the passage can be difficult to apply. I read it, read it again, and asked myself, what does this mean? In general, and specifically, for this moment. I began to break down the scriptures to find an answer. The more I studied, the more I found and the more God gave understanding. And I'd like to share it with you. This book is a breakdown of Proverbs 31:10-31 and suggestions on how you can apply certain actions to achieve being a Proverbs 31 (or P31) woman today, an all-around solid and good human being. Each chapter focuses on one scripture and is designed for you to read one chapter a day. There are suggestions on how to apply the interpretation as well as questions at the end of every chapter to help engage further thought and formulate a game plan to leverage in your own life.

In twenty-two days, learn what it means to be good and how to translate it to your own life. Keep in mind, these are suggestions and tips. Take what may work for you and apply it. If not, no worries, right? Trust me, you'll get something out of it. This is great prep for being a good wife, or ways to improve your role as a wife. The objective is to have a lifestyle of being a genuinely GOOD PERSON, being well-rounded, spreading love in your home, community, and around the world.

STILL I RISE
Dr. Maya Angelou

You may write me down in history
With your bitter, twisted lies,
You may trod me in the very dirt
But still, like dust, I'll rise.

Does my sassiness upset you?
Why are you beset with gloom?
'Cause I walk like I've got oil wells
Pumping in my living room.

Just like moons and like suns,
With the certainty of tides,
Just like hopes springing high,
Still I'll rise.

Did you want to see me broken?
Bowed head and lowered eyes?
Shoulders falling down like teardrops.
Weakened by my soulful cries.

Does my haughtiness offend you?
Don't you take it awful hard
'Cause I laugh like I've got gold mines
Diggin' in my own back yard.

You may shoot me with your words,
You may cut me with your eyes,

You may kill me with you hatefulness,
But still, like air,
I'll rise.

Does my sexiness upset you?
Does it come as a surprise
That I dance like I've got diamonds
At the meaning of my thighs?

Out of the huts of history's shame,
I rise
Up from a part that's rooted in pain,
I rise
I'm a black ocean, leaping and wide,
Welling and swelling I bear in the tide.

Leaving behind nights of terror and fear,
I rise
Into a daybreak that's wondrously clear,
I rise

Bringing the gifts that my ancestors gave,
I am the dream and the hope of the slave.
I rise
I rise
I rise.

THE GOOD WOMAN

"Turn from evil and do good; seek peace and pursue it."
-PSALM 34:14 (NIV)

I have often wondered what one defines as good. Is it based on experience, culture, family, opinion or the Bible? Good vs. Evil? What is the measuring stick and what is the rule of thumb? Is something that is not good, defined as bad or evil? According to whom?

The dictionary defines *good* (adjective) as: to be desired or approved of; what is morally right; righteousness (noun).

What is *righteousness*? The same dictionary says it is the quality of being morally right or justifiable.

To be *moral* is to be concerned with the principles of right and wrong behavior and the goodness or badness of human character. *Right*, morally good, justified or acceptable.

Now, let's consider the word wrong. *Wrong* is defined as: not correct or true.; unjust, dishonest or immoral. "But you must not eat from the tree of the knowledge of good and evil, for when you eat from it you will certainly die," Genesis 2:17 (NIV). There is an acknowledgement of good and evil in the beginning chapters of the Bible. It was commanded not to eat from the tree. This is also an opportunity to be obedient. Instead, there was a lack of trust as well as the notion that God was keeping something good from Adam and Eve. Genesis 2:25 (NIV) says, "Adam and his wife both naked, and they felt no shame." The brief story of deception and the fall are in the early verses of chapter three. We know how that ends. "Then the eyes of both of them were opened, and they realized they were naked; so they sewed fig leaves together and made coverings for themselves," Genesis 3:7 (NIV). The absence of trust and obedience left them exposed. They were exposed to evil. They were living a sin-free life. Things were good, really good, in Eden ("garden of delight") without a need or want. They had one rule to follow and couldn't do that. Do not eat of the tree of the knowledge of good and evil (the first mention of good and it's opposite, evil).

I believe this is what can happen in life. You jump the gun because you can't wait on God. Instead of consulting Him and putting total faith and trust in Him, you do what you want. Of course, because He gave you free will. For you, it may be the road you can't go down, the guy you must stay away from, the crowd to avoid, the music you shouldn't listen to, the food you shouldn't eat. You do what you want regardless of what you have been instructed to do. You make your own choice and sometimes that may harm you, or be things you may not be ready for, things God is preparing you for later. You do it and it's the wrong move. If you have been instructed not to do a specific thing, it puts distance between you and God and separates you from His love and fellowship.

Back to the tree, the forbidden tree, and good versus evil. To be good is to be righteous. To be righteous is to be right. But what they did was wrong. They were instructed not to eat of the tree. Though they were naked, they were good because they had done no wrong, they were "clothed" in righteousness. Metaphorically speaking, though they were naked physically, they were protected from sin because of the righteousness of God. God was their protector. When they didn't do as instructed, they came out from His covering and they knew it right away. They were not protected. They were no longer clothed in righteousness. They were ashamed and resorted to leaves and figs to hide their distinguishing male and female body parts, a physical sign of sin.

I challenge you to read and study the first few chapters of Genesis. As the beginning, it lays the foundation. It will help you better understand sin nature, temptation, deception, blame, accountability, disobedience, shame, life, death, and the introduction to good versus evil. There are some things you do naturally because it's been passed down through sin nature and it may help clarify things for you.

Within each chapter, I will provide an interpretation or breakdown of the material for easy consumption.

INTERPRETATION

To be righteous is to be good. To be good is to morally do right and not wrong. To do and be the opposite of bad and immoral. For an even further interpretation, let's go to the manuscript. Philippians 4:8 (NIV) reads, "Finally, brothers and sisters, whatever is true, whatever is noble, whatever is right, whatever is pure, whatever is lovely, whatever is admirable, if anything is excellent or praiseworthy, think about such things."

To think, to meditate on these things, these good things that will then manifest themselves in your life. Think about positive things and positive things will come to you, by mere law of attraction. It is the same principle described in Matthew 7:7-8 (NIV), "Ask and it will be given to you; seek and you will find; knock and the door will be opened to you. For everyone who asks receives; the one who seeks finds; and to the one who knocks; the door will be opened." You ask, you receive. You seek, you find. You knock, open sesame. Be good and goodness will come back to you.

God is good. I believe that should be the moral standard in which to pattern your life. You were made in His image. Designed for a reason, it is up to you to discover how to live. He sent His son to be a model, that wonderful human being, to show His creation how to be good. They just couldn't get it right and chose not to live according to His instructions and because of that, He had to make the ultimate sacrifice.

> "Why do you ask me about what is good?" Jesus replied. "There is only One who is good. If you want to enter life, keep the commandments."
> **-MATTHEW 19:17 (NIV)**

"Give thanks to the Lord, for he is good; his love endures forever," Psalm 107:1 (NIV). God is good and that is how to become good. If He is the moral compass of good and righteousness, you have the ability to be the same, right? Follow His commandments and live life unto Him and practice it daily. Blessed are the pure in heart for they shall see God. Pretty simple, right?

> "The fear of the Lord is the beginning of knowledge: but fools despise wisdom and instruction."
> **-PROVERBS 1:7 (KJV)**

EVE, THE WOMAN:

God created man in His own image. Male and female created he them (Genesis 1:27). He put both in one body, but both spirits and characteristics were housed/lived in man. Adam-made red hue, Human. Man-mind, God in the flesh. Woman was the manifestation of female in the flesh. He took the female out of Adam. She is the giver of life, can translate to be both physical and spiritual. Wisdom is female. The Holy Spirit is female. God brought her unto the man. Adam was in a deep sleep (during the deep stages of NREM sleep, the body repairs and regrows tissues, builds bone and muscle, and strengthens the immune system. Dreams happen in REM (rapid eye movement) because your brain is more active), which may represent unconsciousness. It is not stated whether Adam woke up, just that woman was brought to man by God. Which brings me to believe that female is a representation of the Kingdom of God. The spirit of God. Woman gives life. Woman, the "weaker vessel," should be protected, held in high regard. Genesis 2:24 reads, "Therefore shall a man leave his father and his mother, and shall cleave unto his wife: and they shall be one flesh." One flesh represents the Kingdom of God. You can't have one without the other, man and woman. Woman's vital role is her representation of the Kingdom. Man was missing one thing, woman, and if woman represents the Kingdom, he is "complete" with woman making them one flesh. She is what he lacks. His inability to see that is the difference between consciousness and unconsciousness.

Adam never "woke up" thus remaining unconscious. He was to protect the sacredness and beauty of woman but instead, he exposed her to evil. He didn't realize his role as it relates to her. He wasn't aware of woman's power to connect to the Kingdom, to the spirit, because woman was new to him. His new assignment, to be a protector of the spirit to protect good, to be righteous. Male's important role is to protect, to keep sacred, honor and love. "Husbands love your wives as Christ loves the church," says Ephesians 5:25. The church (the body of Christ, Christ is God's son in the flesh so when speaking about "the body" of Christ, the church body is God in the flesh) or The Kingdom. "Man is to love his wife/woman" is a direct correlation in the flesh as to how he should respond and treat God. He is her spiritual covering. Covering is defined as a thing used to cover something else, typically in order to protect or conceal it. If man is a spiritual cover to woman, he is protecting her spirit, deeper than that, he is the protector of the spirit, The Kingdom, God's word, and righteousness.

Woman represents the spirit, God in the flesh. Woman is the female side of

God. The spirit is considered female with the understanding of the Father→ Son (male)→ Spirit (female). If you take a rib, the rib cage is used to protect the organs, a covering, which in essence, is key in terms of its functionality. That rib is molded into woman. He took a piece of the "covering" and made woman. Because she is female, she represents the spirit. Now man's new assignment is to cover her spirit. Because she is the representation of God, he is to keep God's spirit from evil. He is to protect, he is to cover.

Creating woman is the physical example, the first physical example, God gave man to try and model. It was God's first test in stewardship. Adam had the whole animal and creatures thing down pat. Woman was the new test. The assignment—to see Adam's loyalty to God. Adam didn't cover and protect woman, the spirit, what was holy and righteous. You can't protect something you're not aware of, something you're not conscious of. You're living in a state of unconsciousness. You're asleep, not awake.

After woman was created, it went wrong rather quickly. After the "fall," they knew they were naked. To be naked is to be without clothing literally but figuratively speaking, it is to be vulnerable, to be free, unrestricted. It represented righteousness; righteousness is immortal. God's intention was for His creation to live forever. But, "The wages of sin is death..." (Romans 6:23). The "fall" was the first exposure to sin. It was the gateway to evil and generations of sin and death. It was not the Creator's intention for us. Instead of passing down righteousness, we've passed down sin, generational curses, issues, and the only way to turn away from that is to live a sinless life. To follow His laws and commandments. To model Christ—the best and most recent example of how to live in righteousness.

Good, righteous, moral, right...and then there is *virtue*, behavior showing high moral standards. To possess and embody virtue you must be good. A good or useful quality of a thing. A quality considered morally good or desirable in a person. *Standard* is a level of quality or attainment. Or a required or agreed level of quality. An idea or thing used as a measure, norm, or model in comparative evaluations. What is the *moral* standard? I believe the moral standard is spiritually-based and starts with God and simply following His commandments. But for the sake of definition, *the level or quality in which you are concerned with the principles of right and wrong behavior. Holding or manifesting high principles for proper conduct.* It is one thing to want to do right, it's another to actually do

> "She is the crescendo, the final, astonishing work of God. Woman. In one last flourish creation came to a finish with Eve. She is the Master's finishing touch."
>
> JOHN ELDREDGE

so. In essence, having a standard and not applying it is like saying you're going to do something and then not doing it. Actions speak louder than words or in this case, standards. To have *virtue* is to behave with a high level of concern for the principles of proper conduct. You are behaving in a high moral standard. The moral standard is God. I don't know how much higher you can go. God is good. And to live a life of virtue is to be like God, made in His image and for His purpose.

Virtuous is having or showing high moral standards. This word is usually associated with women but it is clearly for everyone based on the breakdown of definitions. So, in this case, a virtuous woman is one who is good. A good and noble woman is one who applies the principles of God to her life. A noble woman is Proverbs 31:10-31. She embodies good. The number one thing she does is take care of her family. Her first title even before Adam named her in the Bible was wife. The point of husband and wife is to create a family that is morally good to influence others to be morally good, ultimately for the upbuilding of God's Kingdom. There is a purpose for everyone to live out but the roles as a woman and wife are specific and necessary for the fabric of healthy families. Healthy families create strong communities and unify nations. You, good woman, are a necessity.

Proverbs 31 verses 10-31 is an acrostic poem which means it is a word puzzle. King Solomon, one of the wisest authors of the Bible, wrote the book of Proverbs. However, the last chapter, chapter 31, begins with King Lemuel's mother speaking knowledge about kingly conduct. The gear shifts a bit at verse ten and the chapter and subsequent book of Proverbs reaches its grand finale with a poem about a good woman, a unicorn of a woman, a rare breed, a gem, a jewel, starting off the series with the question: "A wife of noble character who can find?" Perhaps this insert from King Lemuel's mother was passed down to King Solomon. "Here is *Being a King 101*, do's and don'ts just so you know King Solomon." Or maybe it was inserted because of his conduct and inability to control his lust. The passage in Chapter 31 first talks about kingly conduct verses 1-9 and are then followed by this poetry recital of a virtuous woman in verses 10-31. In my research, it's not clear who wrote this specific chapter. Regardless, this specific portion of the book of Proverbs is significant for both men and women.

The chapter includes an intense breakdown of a virtuous woman. A woman of virtue that I believe is a direct correlation to Eve and the garden, God's true intention for woman's role. The most important relationship outside of a personal and intimate relationship with God is that of a spouse. In this case, a husband and Proverbs 31:10-31 describes her in a poem. Not only did God save woman for last in terms of creation, but the passage is in a book possibly from one of the world's wisest men, King Solomon, all to describe how the woman should pattern her life. Welcome to an entire book on the poem, Proverbs 31:10-31, including an interpretation and great suggestions on how to apply it to your life. Welcome to the *Rise of the Good Woman*!

PROVERBS 31: A WIFE OF NOBLE CHARACTER
New International Version, Verses 10-31

10. A wife of noble character who can find? She is worth far more than rubies.

11. Her husband has full confidence in her and lacks nothing of value.

12. She brings him good, not harm, all the days of her life.

13. She selects wool and flax and works with eager hands.

14. She is like the merchant ships, bringing her food from afar.

15. She gets up while it is still night; she provides food for her family and portions for her female servants.

16. She considers a field and buys it; out of her earnings she plants a vineyard.

17. She sets about her work vigorously; her arms are strong for her tasks.

18. She sees that her trading is profitable, and her lamp does not go out at night.

19. In her hand she holds the distaff and grasps the spindle with her fingers.

20. She opens her arms to the poor and extends her hands to the needy.

21. When it snows, she has no fear for her household; for all of them are clothed in scarlet.

22. She makes coverings for her bed; she is clothed in fine linen and purple.

23. Her husband is respected at the city gate, where he takes his seat among the elders of the land.

24. She makes linen garments and sells them, and supplies the merchants with sashes.

25. She is clothed with strength and dignity; she can laugh at the days to come.

26. She speaks with wisdom, and faithful instruction is on her tongue.

27. She watches over the affairs of her household and does not eat the bread of idleness.

28. Her children arise and call her blessed; her husband also, and he praises her:

29. "Many women do noble things, but you surpass them all."

30. Charm is deceptive, and beauty is fleeting; but a woman who fears the Lord is to be praised.

31. Honor her for all that her hands have done, and let her works bring her praise at the city gate.

THE GOOD WOMAN
Questions

How would you define good?

_____

_____

_____

How would you define righteousness?

_____

_____

_____

What is the significance of the story of the tree of good and evil?

_____

_____

_____

How do you believe God is good?

_____

_____

_____

Read Matthew 19:17. What do you take from the passage?

_____

_____

_____

Should virtue and good start with the woman? Why or why not?

_____

_____

_____

Do you believe you are good?

_____

_____

_____

What changes can you make to be a better woman?

_____

_____

_____

_____

What can you do to make this world good?

_____

_____

_____

Books:
Captivating by John Eldredge
And Still I Rise by Maya Angelou

Bonus Comments:

_____

_____

_____

_____

_____

_____

RISE

of the

Good
woman

A wife of noble
character who can find?
She is worth far more than
rubies."

1

KNOW YOUR WORTH

> Verse 10: "A wife of noble character who can find? She is worth far more than rubies."

Interpretation: Perhaps a rhetorical question, who can find a noble or virtuous woman? Solomon, the very wise King, is asking the question because he had not come across a virtuous woman. In Ecclesiastes 7:28 (NIV) he says, "While I was still searching but not finding I found one upright man among a thousand, but not one upright woman among them all." So, he was searching and had yet to come across one upright woman. Because of this, the value of a virtuous woman was far above that of rubies. It was as if he was looking for a unicorn. Oh, they don't exist, he discovered. And this is after Proverbs 31 so perhaps there may have been some frustration about finding a good and noble woman. I can only imagine the women throwing themselves at him because after all, this is Solomon. Solomon, the man of many women, couldn't find a good one. Makes you think, right? He couldn't find one so that doesn't necessarily mean they didn't exist. He's just one guy. However, he was wise so I'm sure his level of discernment was extreme. So, to find a good woman is like finding a treasure box full of rubies. Rubies that are the crown of her husband. Keep reading.

> "A wise woman makes for a jewel of an excellent wife. She sparkles brilliantly."
>
> -RAYMOND E. LLOYD JR.

THE GEM: THE RUBY

According to the International Gem Society, rubies have many associations with power, wealth, and protection. Red in color, it symbolizes blood, the life sustaining fluid. The queen of stones worn by Kings. A ruby has always been a talisman (an object, typically an inscribed ring or stone, that is thought to have magic powers and to bring good luck) of passion, protection and prosperity. Worn as a charm to ward off plagues and pestilence, it warned of danger, kept the body safe, banished sadness and foolish thoughts. Meant to bring peace, drive away frightful dreams, restrain lust, help to resolve disputes. The value of this stone was as high as it's symbolism and purpose.

Let's break this gem down. Blood is a fluid necessary for humans to function. When you are a queen, you rule with the king. A lucky charm. It rids you of bad things and protects you. Gives you passion and prosperity, drives away sadness, frightful dreams and foolish thoughts. Helps resolve disputes and restrains lust. What a stone!

Modern-day rubies aren't as popular as diamonds. In Western society, diamonds are believed to be the most valuable stone or gem. History Fact: In the late 1940's, The De Beers Group financed by the Rothschild (at the time one of the wealthiest families in the world) and Oppenheimer families (sold share of De Beers in 2012 but still extremely wealthy) used a marketing strategy as a way to take over the diamond industry by selling the princess jewel fantasy with its slogan, "A Diamond is Forever." It became popular causing a saturation of the stone that is still used today. Due to effective positioning and marketing by two world-dominating families, the diamond has become the man-made symbol that represents a man's love for his darling. Diamonds are forever, perhaps not. It is a gem that losses its value after purchase. Try pawning a diamond ring. In addition, the stone is known to cause harm (blood diamonds). So, although the diamond is still a nice stone, its value is not comparable to that of a ruby. We must give the RUBY its do and Biblical significance.

> "Wisdom is better than rubies.
> All desires are not to be compared to it."
> **PROVERBS 8:11 (KJV)**

In order to really understand the "ruby" symbolism in this scripture, one must ask what is above rubies? What is far above rubies? A good woman and wisdom. Shut your mouth! Yes, it is so far up there! To be a good woman is invaluable, it is priceless, it is divine, it is EVERYTHING.

EVERYTHING!

> "For wisdom is more profitable than silver, and her wages are better than gold. Wisdom is more precious than rubies; nothing you desire can compare with her."
> **PROVERBS 3:14-15 (KJV)**

Let's talk wisdom. The Hebrew word *hokmah* means wisdom or skill for living. It is the formula to a life of fulfillment and purpose. If you despise wisdom, you disagree with the proper way to conduct your life according to God's principals and instruction. God = good. In essence you go against good. What is the opposite of good, well, evil.

> "Fear of the Lord is the foundation of true wisdom. All who obey his commandments will grow in wisdom."
> **PSALMS 111:10 (NLT)**

WISDOM

"Woman is also a representation of wisdom. Wisdom is considered female/her/she. Just like the man is to cover and protect the spirit, he is to do the same for wisdom.

The woman is the flesh example or representation of God's spirit and wisdom! And that, along with her beauty, make her a force not to be compared to. She is hands down the best thing God created. She is closest to God. Not only is she the giver of life, she's a beauty, alluring in her mind, soul and physicality. She is mesmerizing and The Creator's most beautiful masterpiece. The envy of the enemy. You don't think that the enemy was jealous of someone more beautiful than him? He sought to destroy her. The attack of a woman's beauty is a trick of the enemy. You break her down, it's the downfall of humankind of mother earth...the giver of life. Man's duty is to honor, protect and love woman...as he loves woman he loves The Father. It's love for God in action."

"The fear of the Lord is the beginning of wisdom: and knowledge of the holy is understanding." Proverbs 9:10 (KJV)

"Wisdom makes one wise person more powerful than ten rulers in a city."
Ecclesiastes 7:19 (NIV)

Excerpt from Proverbs 2 (NIV)
Moral benefits of Wisdom:

"1 My son, if you accept my words and store up my commends within you, 2 turning your ear to wisdom and applying your heart to understanding 3 indeed, if you call out for insight and cry aloud for understanding, 4 and if you look for it as for silver and search for it as for hidden treasure, 5 then you will understand the fear of the Lord and find the knowledge of God. 6 For the Lord gives wisdom; from his mouth come knowledge and understanding. 7 He holds success in store for the upright, he is a shield to those whose walk is blameless, 8 for he guards the course of the just and protects the way of his faithful ones. 9 Then you will understand what is right and just and fair- every good path. 10 For wisdom will enter your heart, and knowledge will be pleasant to your soul. 11 Discretion will protect you, and understanding will guard you. 12 Wisdom will save you from the ways of wicked men, from men whose word are perverse, 13 who have left the straight paths to walk in dark ways, 14 who delight in doing wrong and rejoice in the perverseness of evil, 15 whose paths are crooked and who are devious in their ways. 16 Wisdom will save you also from the adulterous woman, from the wayward woman with her seductive words, 17 who has left the partner of her youth and ignored the covenant she made before God. 18 Surely her house leads down to death and her paths to the spirits of the dead. 19 None who go to her return or attain the paths of life. 20 Thus you will walk in the ways of the good and keep to the paths of the righteous. 21 For the upright will live in the land, and the blameless will remain in it; 22 but the wicked will be cut off from the land, and the unfaithful will be torn from it."

Um, hello! Wisdom is more precious than rubies and a virtuous woman is far above rubies. So, she is somewhere between wisdom and rubies. Dear GOOD woman, you are INVALUABLE. You are necessary for the function of God's original intention of good before sin and evil corrupted the earth, before humans were tainted with sin nature.

Wisdom
Noble/Virtuous Woman
Rubies

> "You're trying to get someone to fall in love with a you that you've never discovered yourself."
>
> -TD JAKES

APPLYING: KNOW YOUR WORTH.

YOU ARE PRICELESS. It is important for you to know your worth. This good and noble woman was held in high esteem. Can you be compared to that of a ruby? It was the stone of all stones. To know your worth, you have to know yourself. You have to know who God created you to be. In order to figure that out, you have to have a personal relationship with God. Spending quality alone time with God, lots of alone time as well as therapeutic time alone, to work on you.

> "Wisdom, like an inheritance, is a good thing and benefits those who see the sun."
>
> ECCLESIASTES 7:11 (NIV)

SACRED TIME.

This means specifically taking the time out to get to know yourself. You will not have a clue as to the value you possess if you don't know who you are. In order to come to that revelation, time is required and self-realization is the objective. *Self-realization* is the fulfillment of one's own potential. If you don't take time to figure out what you are capable of, you have yet to reach your full potential. You have not reached your purpose and God's intention for your life. Your true authentic worth is there. You can then make decisions based upon your value as it allows the space for your worth to go before you. The results, you will not so much as entertain specific things when you know your worth. You won't go certain places when you know the value of self. You will refrain from being around certain people and energy.

> "We are a weak society until women realize how powerful they are."
> **TONY GASKINS**

WHAT WENT WRONG

"Oh my, oh my how we've gotten it all wrong and messed things up. I'm a huge fan of getting to know who you are and God's will and purpose for your life. However, focus on career has taken over. It's a huge distraction becauOh my, oh my, how we've gotten it all wrong and messed things up. I'm a huge fan of getting to know who you are and God's will and purpose for your life. However, focus on career has taken over. It's a huge distraction because the busier you are, doing for "the man," the less attention you give yourself. The less you give yourself, the less you know who you are. This is what is happening with our generation. Not only are people waiting to get married because of careers, they want to wait until they are ready. Buying into the notion of getting to a certain level of success before even considering marriage. Without putting equal, if not more time into knowing who they are, making it extremely difficult to determine what they want in a life partner. The career has turned into purpose. In some cases, a career is not God's purpose for an individual's existence. It's a job, a means to provide the necessary resources to live out your purpose. But we have no clue. Why? Because on top of the distraction of career, add in all the other things that distract—TV, social media, events, sports, etc. Cluttering your life and keeping you far from you. And if one doesn't know who they are, why get married only to lose yourself in the marriage?

"If she's amazing, she won't be easy. If she's easy she won't be amazing. If she's worth it you won't give up. If you give up, you're not worthy." Bob Marley

MINDFUL PROTECTION.

You are amazing. There is so much beauty in getting to the core of who you are and knowing what you have to offer. When you know your worth, you do what you can to protect it. You don't want anyone to come and destroy your awesomeness. No one. Understand this, the enemy takes pride in breaking down the woman. Because if you break down the woman, you disrupt the one who brings life. You slowly eat away at the man and thus break down families leaving the potential of a myriad of troublesome things as a result. Look at our society, look at our children. Make sure you protect your awesomeness.

A broken and wounded woman cannot be what is needed of her for her man. She cannot see past her hurt to see what the man lacks. She is incapable of bringing life, peace, fulfillment and joy because she herself lacks. The helper, ("help meet") indeed needs help herself. She is blinded and subconsciously moves about her life unproductive of her design by God for man. The woman waits to be rescued. Right? For the man to gallop into her life and save her. She is not ready. She's not ready because she looks to man to be her knight in shining armor. The only one that can save her is the one who designed her, God.

The Creator is the only way for a woman to become all she is meant to be. It's not meant for woman to be passive but by being her truest self, she becomes irreplaceable. By becoming who God designed her to be, getting to know herself and discovering her purpose, she can then truly take on her role.

> "No husband in his right mind wants a spineless echo, an unthinking shadow shuffling through the house. He wants one who "crowns" his life, someone who surrounds him with her inner beauty, who adorns his life with gems of efficiency and strength, who adds sparkle and depth and delight to the home."
>
> **RAYMOND E. LLOYD JR.**

> "Ladies a man who knows who he is and where he's going will recognize his need for a helpmeet. You just need to know who you are and what type of man you can help. Then position yourself to be found."
>
> **TERRY STEPHENS II**

START AT THE BEGINNING.

How do you get to know yourself in order to recognize your worth? You must start with your early childhood years. Infant to six years of age are critical and formative years, they should not be taken lightly. Those years are responsible for molding and shaping how you view life. Take a deep look at how you were raised, how you were loved, accepted and treated. What were the key turning points in your life? My parents divorced when I was young, around six. Life was uncertain, inconsistent, confusing and compromising. My brother, sister and I were all over the place. And then my dad remarried and that took on a whole different spin. Adjustment after adjustment whether we liked it or not. That shaped me. I'm still all over the place. It's not a bad thing per se, but I like to be on the go and coupled with my free spirit makes for an interesting combination. I embrace it and love it. To stay still is not me, I'm far from a homebody. Again, start at the beginning.

> "Make sure you don't start seeing yourself through the eyes of people who don't value you. Know your worth even if they don't."
> UNKNOWN

QUESTION EVERYTHING.

Ask yourself what traits and personality do you take from your parents and immediate family. What did you take from those who influenced you the most? Who are you? Really start to ask yourself these questions. What makes me happy? Sad? Why do I react to certain things the way I do? Am I insecure? Why? The answers to your questions can be found on the inside.

> "Truth is not to be found outside. No teacher, no scripture can give it to you. It is inside you and if you wish to attain it, seek your own company. Be with yourself."
> OSHO

Purchase a journal to write everything out. It's the best way to start. Write out questions and answer them without holding back. You already have what it takes to be who God created you to be. You just have to ask Him to reveal it, help develop and walk in your God granted talent or gift. Know who you are. Know your worth.

> "When we are happy and accepting of who we are, it cultivates worthiness and confidence which leads to us making better choices for ourselves."
> **LESLIE NELAND, FINDING MR. FOREVER**

ANSWER THE FOLLOWING QUESTIONS:

What did you dream of doing when you were a child?

_____

_____

_____

_____

From where are you operating—anger, hurt, love, or a different emotion?

_____

_____

_____

_____

What makes you jump in excitement? What stirs your soul?

_____

_____

_____

What is your purpose? Why are you alive?

_____

_____

_____

If money or time were not factors, what would you do with your life?

_____

_____

_____

_____

What would you do if you knew you'd be successful?

_____

_____

_____

_____

Of what are you most proud?

_____

_____

_____

_____

_____

List 5 things you love about yourself:

1. _____

2. _____

3. _____

4. _____

5. _____

List 5 of your strengths:

1. _____

2. _____

3. _____

4. _____

5. _____

List 5 of your weaknesses:

1. _____

2. _____

3. _____

4. _____

5. _____

What makes you unique?

_____

_____

_____

_____

_____

Write 5 words you'd use to describe yourself:

1. _____

2. _____

3. _____

4. _____

5. _____

List 5 of your hobbies:

1. _____

2. _____

3. _____

4. _____

5. _____

Do you allow people, life, and circumstances to deny you of greatness? If so, why and how?

_____

_____

_____

_____

_____

Are you scared of you? Why or why not?

_____

_____

_____

_____

_____

What are 5 things that may be holding you back?

1. _____

2. _____

3. _____

4. _____

5. _____

What are 5 things you should change about yourself?

1. _____

2. _____

3. _____

4. _____

5. _____

What is keeping you from truly getting to know yourself?

_____

_____

_____

_____

_____

_____

What is stopping you from spending time with yourself?

_____

_____

_____

Are you ready to take a leap and move forward?

_____

_____

_____

What do you need to unlearn?

_____

_____

_____

_____

What are 5 things you should do daily?

1. _____

2. _____

3. _____

4. _____

5. _____

Write 5 things you can do by yourself, on a regular basis, to stay in touch with YOU. This is self-care.

1. _____

2. _____

3. _____

4. _____

5. _____

What is your favorite place to escape to?

_____

_____

_____

_____

List 5 things that motivate you:

1. _____

2. _____

3. _____

4. _____

5. _____

Look in the mirror and state why you forgive yourself.

Now, look in the mirror and state what you love about yourself.

Try to repeat this exercise daily.

> "If you are never alone, you can't know yourself."
> -PAULO COELHO

That is just a start to get you in the mindset to ask yourself the right questions. It will cause you to seek answers and that is the objective. Find out who you are, why you do what you do, where you'd like to take your life and what's inside of you. When, what, where, why and how, works every time. You just have to keep searching. It's a constant quest to stay aligned with yourself and The Creator. It can be summed up to self-reflection and consistent self-reflection is a humbling process. It is essential to find out why you think, say and do certain things. It helps in the progress of your life. You learn and grow as you consciously better yourself. When you know who you are, it is easier to make sound decisions because you know what will work for your life, are aware of your truth, and are clear on your life's direction.

> "I am not afraid of my truth anymore, and I will not omit pieces of me to make you comfortable."
> ALEX ELLE

POSITIVE AFFIRMATIONS

I AM BEAUTIFUL

I AM INTELLIGENT

I AM GOOD

I AM SUCCESSFUL

I AM AMAZING

I AM UNIQUE

I AM LOVING

I AM KIND

I AM CONFIDENT

I AM GIVING

I AM A LIGHT BEARER

I AM WORTHY OF ALL GOOD THINGS

I AM COURAGEOUS

I AM STRONG

I AM HEALTHY

I AM RADIANT

I AM CREATIVE

I AM DESIGNED TO PERFECTION

I AM MAKING MY DREAMS COME TRUE

I AM MORE THAN ENOUGH

I AM A CONQUEROR

I AM A SURVIVOR

I AM IN CONTROL OF MY THOUGHTS

I AM ABLE TO MANIFEST MY THOUGHTS

I AM GOD'S GOOD AND PERFECT WILL

I AM HAPPY AND FULL OF JOY

I AM POSITIVE AND IT COMES BACK TO ME

I AM ENERGETIC

I AM GREATER THAN MY CIRCUMSTANCES

I AM BLESSED

I AM NECESSARY

I AM DESIGNED BY GOD FOR A PURPOSE

I AM IN LOVE WITH MYSELF

I AM IN TUNE WITH MYSELF

I AM AT PEACE WITH MYSELF

I AM UNAPOLOGETICALLY ME

I AM LOVED BY THE CREATOR OF ALL

I AM _____

DAY 1
Questions

> Verse 10: "A wife of noble character who can find? She is worth far more than rubies."

What did you learn from the chapter?

_____

_____

_____

_____

How do you view diamonds now?

_____

_____

_____

_____

Do you know your worth? Do you believe you are priceless? A rare gem?

_____

_____

_____

Did your perception of women change after reading this chapter? If so, in what way?

_____

_____

_____

Can you confidently say you truly know yourself? How?

_____

_____

_____

Do you spend time alone? What do you do during that time?

_____

_____

_____

What was your first impression of love? Did you learn to appreciate your uniqueness at a young age (5-10)?

_____

_____

_____

_____

Make a list of things you can do to know yourself better:

_____

_____

_____

Create your own list of affirmations using the previous list for inspiration. Type or write them and make a habit of reading them aloud at least once a day. Say them with confidence. More importantly, believe them with all of your heart. Have fun.

I AM _____

I AM _____

I AM _____

I AM _____

I AM _____

Books:

Mrs. Right by Tony Gaskins

Finding Mr. Forever by Leslie Neland

Manuscript Found in Accra by Paulo Coelho

Woman, Thou Art Loosed by TD Jakes

The Black Girl's Guide to Being Blissfully Feminine by Candice Adewole

A Woman's Worth by Marianne Williamson

Becoming Myself: Embracing God's Dream of You by Stasi Eldredge

The Truth About Men by Devon Franklin

Today I Affirm: A Journal that Nurtures Self-Care by Alexandra Elle

Bonus Comments:

_____

_____

_____

Her husband has full confidence in her and **lacks nothing** of value.

2

BE FEMININE

Verse 11: "Her husband has full confidence in her and lacks nothing of value."

Interpretation: She has proven herself to be loyal, honest and true to him. Her husband has full trust in her. The heart of her husband believes in her ability to succeed on his behalf and the family. She adds to his life. No lack of gain. He has no need because she takes care of him. He won't lack anything of value. *Value*, the regard to something that is held to deserve. Of importance, worth or usefulness. He has full confidence in her loyalty. She is gentle and kind, not spiteful.

APPLYING: BE FEMININE.

Feminine is having qualities or appearance traditionally associated with women, especially delicacy and prettiness. Synonyms: womanly, ladylike, girlish, soft, gentle, delicate, graceful. *Delicacy*, fineness or intricacy of texture or structure. *Masculine* is defined as having qualities or appearance traditionally associated with men, especially strength and aggressiveness.

To be feminine is to really be the opposite of male. To be what he doesn't already have or possess. To be feminine is to embody your function as a woman and in this case, a wife. The woman in this passage is the same and given the title of wife in Genesis. She is a help-meet. To help and assist your husband is your primary function as his wife. It is to be what he lacks. A woman/wife is what man/husband is missing. There is a uniqueness that a woman brings otherwise God would have made more

"To me a lady is not frilly, flouncy, flippant, frivolous and fluff-brained, but she is gentle. She is gracious. She is godly and she is giving. You and I have the gift of femininity...the more womanly we are, the more manly men will be and the more God is glorified. Be women, be only women. Be real women in obedience to God."

ELISABETH ELLIOT

men. He realized there was and still is a necessity for more than the male species. They need us, your husband needs you.

Being feminine or to display femininity is the quality of being female. Womanly, ladylike, delicate, etc. It is energy, an energy that needs to be tapped into. The energy that naturally makes you a woman. Like the Holy Spirit, she is a comforter, she is to be the calming of a storm. Soothing, supportive and what he doesn't have. Breathe life into him. It is your duty to take on the spirit of God, the consciousness of The Father in a gentle and subtle manner. The flow of the spirit should move you euphorically. Motivate him, be his biggest cheerleader...all the time. Allow the man to be the man. He is a protector, provider, trainer, teacher, a guide. But he needs you, and tapping into your femininity will remind him why.

I love this post from the lovely, April Mason written specifically for Black women. It's so good, I had to include.

"Being strong and independent by societies [sic] definition is NOT a badge of honor. We have been programmed to believe that we don't need anything or anybody, especially a man. I don't know about you, but I don't want to be strong and carry it all. Yes, I understand that we've had too [sic] in order to take care of our families. Well, I say NO MORE! Men get in your rightful positions and women LET THEM! We are breaking our bodies down having to do it

all. We haven't a clue about our purpose because our lives have been dedicated to taking care of others and not ourselves."

"Back hurting, knees bad, arms weak and health issues all because of the pride associated with being called "a strong black woman." Our strength is in our FEMININITY, but we have LOST or never even tapped into it because we've been trained to be strong in a masculine sense. Who cares why it happened, it's time to fix it! NO MORE BLAME! NO MORE EXCUSES! IT'S TIME TO HIT THE RESET BUTTON! Time to get back to being a feminine woman! My message is for the group of women who understand their place and have no problem taking it."

God gave women such great qualities, our natural ability to nurture and our intuition are two of the best in my opinion. *Intuition* is a feeling that connects the soul to the brain. *Female Intuition*, is the ability to be in tune with your emotions. Your emotions take on many different forms and there are different ways in which to express them. Women are great communicators. And the way in which you articulate those emotions, the more in touch you are with the power of femininity. The emotions that stir up in your soul should not be ignored.

> "God gave women intuition and femininity. Used properly, the combination easily jumbles the brain of any man I've ever met."
> FARRAH FAWCETT

PLAYING THE ROLE:

"Role play, better to call it God's design for woman. Giver of life, nurturer, beauty, alluring in her mind, soul and physicality. The companion, the rock, the confidante, the reasoning, the motivation. She is feminine. She is mesmerizing. The envy of the enemy. The Creator's most beautiful masterpiece. The best, He saved for last. Let's just be real, there are far more beautiful women than handsome men. God truly had the man in mind when He created woman. The attack of a woman's beauty is a trick of the enemy. You break her down, it's the downfall of humankind."

"It's not meant for woman to be passive but by being her truest self, she

becomes irreplaceable. Alluring and not just with outer beauty because you can be beautiful on the outside and ugly, really awful, on the inside. Who wants a woman that's ugly on the inside? It cancels out the external beauty."

"The average modern woman is too concerned with physical appearance that she doesn't do the work on the inside. She is too busy trying to seduce and allure with what she puts on, the time is never devoted to become who she is designed to be. She walks around with a heavy load, invisible baggage. She masks the pain and hurt inside, never dealing with the experiences that plague her insecurities. Her mommy and daddy issues, the lack of validation, trust, abuse in all forms, she ignores her lack. It's hidden in a designer handbag. She carries her BAGgage on her shoulders walking with hips swaying left to right, to allure. To allure with her body because she believes that it's the way to validate her worth. It's in the lipstick and foundation she smears on her face each day. The eye make-up to cover up the gateway to her soul. It's a cover up, she's a Cover-Girl. She brings all the boys to the yard. She got that milk with her shake, she can easily fool an unwise man. Her hurt and pain, she'll internalize. She'll put on enough to convince some man she is worthy of his love. She marries and then wants her man to fulfill her lack, to carry her BAGgage for her. Man, perplexed and confused about the woman he thought he chose, after the bags are dropped and the make-up is off. She does not know who she is, who she was truly designed to be and the rescuer she claims to know."

WAYS TO EXERCISE YOUR FEMININITY:

BE GRACEFUL. To be graceful is elegance, a quality of being stylish in appearance or in manner. It's the difference between dinnerware from Target and fine china. Like ten dollar wine versus wine that has gone through a long fermentation process and cost a couple hundred dollars. It is the way you walk, talk, smile, gesture and embrace. It's inviting with pleasantries of your personality. It is the energy you carry and sprinkle around everywhere you go. The way you leave people long after you've left their physical presence. It is entering a room and people being awestruck that you have appeared. It is warmth, gentleness, unassuming yet all so gravitating. It is a magnetic force that even the most mean and evil spirited cannot help but take a bow to its power. To be graceful is to be feminine. It is the foundation of femininity. It is the stability of what it is to be feminine.

> "Males will not feel comfortable making significant investment in a female who runs off at the mouth or who is not good at expressing herself."
> **KONGIT FARRELL**

BE CALM. Be soft and gentle. Your husband has the responsibility of being 1) The spiritual leader of the household. Your spiritual covering specifically. 2) Protector, physically as well as emotionally. 3) Provider. Sole provider of the house. It's a lot and the more understanding you have, the better. By being calm, soft, and gentle, you help to create a space of comfort. I call it being pink. Being pink is being soft. People associate pink with girls, especially as babies. We are strong yet delicate. And in the presence of men, women should be calm and delicate and allow them to be strong and protective. Being calm is like solace to a man. It celebrates their manhood, they can take over without contest or issue. And by no means am I saying you don't have a voice, chill out and be calm. It's usually not that deep. Let him take the lead.

> "Might we not be fooled into thinking that love will only meet us if we are docile, shy and a whisper. We don't have to brag or boast or be cocky, but strength, boss and empowered are the beautiful terms that describe a creative, beautiful, attractive, virtuous woman."
> **CHRISETTE MICHELLE**

Excerpt from *The Black Girl's Guide to Being Blissfully Feminine* by Candice Adewole:

"As women, we have so much power with our words and the sounds of our voices. Our words and voices are two of the ways we can nurture those around us. Men use the tone and inflection of our voices to gauge whether we are pleased, whether we can be pleased, or whether they want to bother trying to please us at all. We can build up or tear down with our words. I believe that every woman has a girly, feminine voice. This is the soft voice we use when talking to babies and animals, or when talking over the phone to that guy who makes our hearts race. This is the voice we should use most of the time."

BE FEMININE. There are such wonderful things that make women different than men. It is up to you to make sure the line isn't crossed. And as a wife, being in touch with your feminine side is key. A lot of being female has to do with clothing. What you wear and how you wear it can be the difference between exhibiting masculinity or femininity. Women are easily identified by dresses. I'm not saying go back to the days of dresses and skirts only but it's not a bad thing.

I don't own sweatsuits. I have been wearing leggings and yoga pants for more than a decade. Joggers are a stretch as the droopy middle is not attractive. Put something cute on all the time, even a tank dress can be sexy. There are child appropriate house-roaming clothes you can put on per your body type. Try crop tops, off-the shoulder shirts, high shorts or boy shorts. Anything see-through is always going to catch his eye. Lounging in big t-shirts, sweats, or otherwise is masculine. Exceptions would be wearing one of his dress shirts as a dress. The point is to give him female, lots of female. More dresses and skirts over pants and pantsuits or masculine looking clothing. Overall, wear what makes you feel sexy, if you feel sexy you will exude sexiness.

Sistas, no rags on your head either. Try headbands or scarf headbands (like patterned bandanas), anything else is a turn off. I haven't worn a scarf on my head for a good ten years just headbands as it makes me feel sexy. I sleep by myself each night (for now) but believe you can always be sexy for yourself. Now, about those head scarfs (I'm not touching the bonnet), you have to figure it out on your own. Please know that it is a huge turn off for men. When they roll over, they want to see something attractive and appealing. You can't really do a whole lot with bed hair but try more often than not to be alluring in bed. Be sexy and not like you are going to an all-girl slumber party.

I read somewhere that you should never look better outside of the house than you do inside. In essence, you should want to look good for your husband and impress him rather than all of the people you see outside that could not care less. Wear heals, accessories, earrings, bracelets, get your nails, toes and hair done. Accentuate your assets in modesty. A feminine woman is a classy lady. Act like you care and put forth effort to be a beautiful wife for him. Represent him well.

> "Men love sexy, flowing dresses and vibrant colors. Anything that shows your femininity is a keeper."
> LESLIE NELAND, FINDING MR. FOREVER

BE VULNERABLE. When in the presence of a man, ask for help. Be the damsel in distress more often than not. Let your husband save you. I practice this now, when a man is around, I make it a point to politely ask for things. *Can you pass me that? I'm sorry, can you help me with this?* I am working hard to reverse doing everything for myself as an independent woman. I don't want to do everything myself and I understand that I need help. So, admitting you need assistance is okay. Trying to do everything all the time is insane. Being open to asking for help is the hardest part but once you get used to it, it's delightful.

Being vulnerable is also about staying in touch with your emotions. I've heard emotion described as energy in motion. It is the manifestation of the energy you have inside displaying on the outside, e-motion. That is the beauty of being female, the ability to be in tune with what is felt. If the connection of energy is understood, it is easier to communicate. That communication and expression is something very unique and more likely to come from the woman than the man. Open yourself to be in your feelings and be vulnerable. But make sure that you express them with gentleness and kindness.

> "The feminine is more powerful than the masculine, the soft is more powerful than the hard, the water is more powerful than the rock."
> OSHO

STAY FRESH. Personal hygiene is a must. But more than anything, smelling pleasant arouses the senses and is also feminine. I'm all for natural products like essential oils as they are a healthier alternative to perfumes. Mist or essential oils mixed with a carrier oil are delightful and best for the body over time. Scents like lavender and lemongrass are enchanting. Either way you to choose to go, smelling good is a necessity.

When I'm out and about, I always carry adult wipes because you never know when you'll need to freshen up. Trying to get to a shower might be difficult and these wipes do the job. There are also feminine wipes that help keep you fresh in your sacred yoni spot when needed. They are small, can fit in a clutch or crossbody, and are great for transitioning from day to night if you can't take a quick shower. I discovered Goodwipes, alcohol & paraben-free body wipes that are 100% biodegradable, on Amazon and they are wonderful. I met the owners, great people, and purchasing their product is a great way to support a small business and help the environment as well.

Years ago, I heard of a practice called chi yok, it's basically a vagina steam. I went to a Korean spa and sat on a bottomless toilet seat of sorts, like a toilet bucket. Underneath was a steaming pot of water with lavender essential oil added. I was covered with a potato sack that had a hole for my head. I just sat there, putting my head in and out of the potato sack to steam my face as well. I was probably there for about 30-minutes. I left feeling clean, really clean. It's more popular now than it was ten years ago when I first had it done. Check around in your area and see if there is a spa that offers the service. If it is not available at a regular spa check a Korean spa. And you may find some resources online or Amazon as it's becoming *a thing*.

I recently came across Naturotica Wellness (www.naturoticawellness.com), a company offering a number of products including teas, ph balancers, and other products specifically for female intimate areas.

Because a P31 woman is always prepared, I keep an extra everything in my car. From lotion, body oils, deodorant, mist, perfume, panties and feminine wipes, to shampoo and conditioner, it's important to think about the what-if moments. A suggestion is to keep an easily-accessible toiletry bag in your car.

SUGGESTED COMPANIES FOR NATURAL BODY CARE PRODUCTS

Herbivore Botanicals
Dr. Bronner's
The Honey Pot Company
Nubian Heritage
Nene FemHealth
Yes God Wellness
Queen Helene
Sprout Wellness
Weleda
Zion Health
Hello Products
Native
Schmidt's
Tom's
Jason
Crystal
The Healthy Deodorant
Lume Deodorant
Hume Supernatural
Cleo & Coco Deodorant
Each & Every
Empress Body
Blume Natural Products

It is up to women to protect and keep femininity sacred. To embody it because it is under constant attack. The threat to femininity is to destroy the essence of woman and to cut off a portion of God's image. Made in His image, female is the feminine extension of The Creator. Without female, the

"If masculinity has come under assault, femininity has been brutalized. Eve is the crown of creation, remember? She embodies the exquisite beauty and the exotic mystery of God in a way that nothing else in all creation even comes close to. And so she is the special target of the Evil One; he turns his most vicious malice against her. If he can destroy her or keep her captive, he can ruin the story."

JOHN ELDREDGE

Kingdom is incomplete. It is vitally important to remain in your female energy through femininity so God's perfect order will manifest. That is how important being feminine is. Understand you are the giver of life. You are a living, breathing, walking example of God. You were created special in His image, life can only come through you. The function of the female is necessary for this world to exist and life to carry on.

Whether you have had the pleasure of bringing a child into this world or not, you still give life. Be mindful because what you impregnate yourself with, you will give birth to. For example, planting a seed of negativity and allowing it to develop and grow will eventually give birth to a negative life. It is the same with human life. The seed plants, develops, grows, and then is birthed.

> "Yet you are all mental lepers. Your mind is eaten away with negative thoughts. Some of those thrust upon you. Many of these you actually make up, conjure up yourselves, and then harbor and entertain for hours, days, weeks, months, even years...and you wonder why you are sick."
> **NEALE DONALD WALSH, CONVERSATIONS WITH GOD**

The mother's role is so important in carrying the baby, she has to be aware of what she does during development as well as spirits, traits (generational issues) and emotions. She must be careful as to what she passes down subconsciously. This is where the enemy can attack during pregnancy, postpartum and as children are being raised. It is important to nurture, connect and raise children to be good in order to create good homes, communities and nations. So, femininity is more than dresses, heels, scents and being alluring. It's about order and aligning yourself in the position for your role as a female. It is the most important role created. Something was missing, and then God created female. Own it. Embrace it. Embody it. Manage it properly. Be good about it.

DAY 2
Questions

| Verse 11: "Her husband has full confidence in her and lacks nothing of value."

What did you take from the chapter?

_____

_____

_____

Why do you think God created women?

_____

_____

_____

Did you realize the power of your femininity? If not, what do you know now?

_____

_____

_____

_____

_____

Do you understand the difference between femininity and feminism?

_____

_____

_____

What is it about women that men need?

_____

_____

_____

Is there something you could teach your daughter(s) or a young lady about being feminine? What?

_____

_____

_____

What other ways can you exercise your femininity?

_____

_____

_____

Books:

The Black Girl's Guide to Being Blissfully Feminine by Candice Adewole
Man Leads: Woman Follows, Everyone Wins by Ro Élori Cutno
Devotional & Journal 365 Days to Healing, Blessings, and Freedom by TD Jakes
Free to Be Me: Becoming the Young Woman God Create You to Be by Stasi Eldredge

Bonus Comments:

_____

_____

_____

_____

_____

_____

_____

_____

She brings him good, not harm, all the days of her life.

3

BE GOOD

> Verse 12: "She will do him good, not harm, all the days of her life."

Interpretation: She will do him good not evil as long as she lives. She accepts him for who He is. She speaks good of him and speaks his praises in public. She celebrates him, his accomplishments and successes. She reverences him, she honors him. She will not try to do anything to deliberately harm him, it is pretty much unthinkable. She only, with true intent, brings good to him. She does not bring up the past. She doesn't emasculate him, she is his peace and his comfort.

APPLYING: BE GOOD.

She will do him good. This is applying good intentions for the betterment of your husband and household. I believe that being a wife is just an extension of being a good person. Refer to the Introduction. You can also apply the saying, "Do until others as you would have them do until you." What you give out will come back to you. The more good you give, the more good you get back. In fact, it is the basic law of attraction. The Law of Attraction is the belief that by focusing on a thing, positive or negative, you will then attract that thing back to you. This includes ideas, people, situations and circumstances.

The simplest way to do him good is to do him good. But being good to your husband, in terms of specifics, depends on him. For example, his view of good or good things may vary from yours a bit. Good may mean having dinner ready when he returns home from work. Or good could be no nagging. Good could be contributing financially to the home. Having a clean home all the time. Laying it down in the bedroom could be his version of good. Good could be keeping your matters private and off of social media, from your parents, family members and friends. Again, it just depends on the two of you. Right?

> "What you want, honey, you got it. And what you need, baby, you've got it. All I'm asking for is a little respect when I come home..."
>
> **THE LATE ARETHA FRANKLIN**

Aretha is right, respect is key. Women and men alike want to be respected. That goes along with being good. To reverence him is to honor God. How you treat God is a direct reflection of how you should treat your spouse. This isn't putting him above God but he is to be treated with respect and dignity. It is simply a matter of respect as a wife to her husband.

"Then the Lord God said, "It is not good that he should be alone; I will make him a helper suitable for him." Genesis 2:18 (NIV). Then He created animals and had Adam name them. That wasn't good enough, something was still missing. There is something that a woman brings that ONLY she can. An alluring, softness, pleasantness that differentiates women from men. Offering him what he doesn't have or is in lack of is good. You have to figure out what that means for you and him.

> "But for man no suitable helper was found. So the Lord God caused the man to fall into a deep sleep; and while he was sleeping, he took one of the man's ribs and then closed up the place with flesh. Then the Lord God made a woman from the rib he had taken out of the man, and he brought her to the man."
>
> **GENESIS 2:20-22 (NIV)**

So, the first thing to describe woman was helper. *Help* is to make it easier for someone to do something by offering one's services or resources. Sit on that.

By no means is a wife inferior to her husband. By mere responsibility, the wife is subject to her husband and only to her husband. To be *obedient,* to submit to the will of another. To comply to orders or requests. Keep reading we'll get into this part. Back to this help-meet thing. Help, like assist. This is the first description of woman. To help your husband with pretty much everything is good. Sounds like a team to me. A unit. A kingdom.

> "Therefore shall a man leave his father and his mother, and shall cleave unto his wife: and they shall be one flesh."
> **GENESIS 2:24 (KJV)**

Woman was designed for man. His life was lonely without woman. She is an extension of him. From the rib, bone of bone and flesh of flesh. God presented woman to man. They become one flesh. Woman is to provide companionship and assistance. She is the "Co," the Co-Manager, Co-Pilot, Co-Leader. A woman brings a man what he lacks. This makes "becoming one flesh" accurate. Woman was designed different, she's the other half of man. She brings life. She brings life. She brings life. Life, peace, fulfillment, joy.

God
Man
Woman (Here because of sin)

Let's talk about the sin that led to the current pecking order. Adam claimed woman as "bone of my bones," "flesh of my flesh" which symbolizes equality. There was no division. They were unified through marriage. Walking side by side. And then she was tempted and deceived. She ate the forbidden fruit, convinced Adam to do the same and brought sin and death into human existence. And that is the reason woman went from "walking alongside" man to "walking two steps behind," metaphorically speaking. Genesis 3:16 (KJV) says, "Unto the woman he said, I will greatly multiply thy sorrow and thy conception; in sorrow thou shalt bring forth children; and thy desire shall be to thy husband, and he shall rule over thee." The tendency by nature and design is to walk along with man. But because of the curse and punishment of sin, there is a pecking order. It's not slavery, it's more or less accountability. And that's accountability to your husband, let's be clear. More on that later.

> "You are the producers. You are the ones through whom life passes. Every child who enters into this world must come through you. Even Jesus Christ had to come through you to get legal entry into the world. He had to come through you. You are a channel and an expression of blessings. If there is to be any virtue, any praise, any victory, any deliverance, it's got to come through you."
>
> **TD JAKES**

This is an all-important position. I've heard, the man is the head but the woman is the neck. Let's play with this analogy. He can't move his head without you. Or better, the neck connects the head to the rest of the body. No neck, the rest of the body cannot properly function. Your neck is connected to your spine so in terms of alignment, when your neck is off, the rest of your body is too, including your spine. The spine, and being in complete alignment, can be correlated with your spiritual alignment with The Creator. In marriage, when the head is disconnected from the neck, the neck is off and the marriage isn't aligned with God. Thus, making the marriage off in general.

> "The aged women likewise, that they be in behavior as becometh holiness, not false accusers, not given to much wine, teachers of good things; That they may teach the young women to be sober, to love their husbands, to love their children, To be discreet, chaste, keepers at home, good, obedient to their own husbands, that the word of God be not blasphemed."
>
> **TITUS 3:3-5 (KJV)**

However, if the woman is not doing her part, bringing what the man doesn't have, then your marriage is not whole and you are not one flesh. Why should woman bring what man brings? In essence, it becomes unbalanced. You have two claiming to be one. Having two different agendas or two missions is out of alignment. It eventually equals incompatibility and a disconnect that can lead to the demise of the marriage. Like the garden, Eve was doing her own thing. Adam wasn't "awake" (he was disconnected) to realize he needed to protect her. Through her charm and feminine nature, she easily persuaded Adam to follow suit. And humanity suffers even today.

> "Emasculation lowers a man's testosterone level, which is believed to negatively compromise a man's willpower, his mood, his physical strength, his immune system, his sex drive, his sexual ability, his sperm count, his sperm quality, his work performance, his patience, his nervous system, his self-esteem, and his self-respect. Avoiding emasculation is literally a matter of health."
>
> **RO ÉLORI CUTNO, MAN LEADS: WOMAN FOLLOWS, EVERYONE WINS**

Backbiting, smirking, smacking of lips, raising eyebrows or other gestures that may offend should be avoided especially in public. Think of how a Queen conducts herself toward her King. She is often silent, in public. I'm not saying women don't have a voice. I'm simply saying that the way in which we speak should be calculated, wise, and uplifting. Voicing your concerns or opinions can be done but always from a space of love and gentleness and reserved for private. A woman should always come from a place of nurturing therefore, it is soft and kind. Men and children are both able to receive what is being communicated. And I must say that this is hard when emotions are high and egos are bruised. Try your best to keep your composure. I love how Claire Huxtable (The Cosby Show) handled things. Her tone was leveled but her words were powerful. When I think tone and getting a point across, I hear Claire's voice loud and clear. She didn't play but she was also feminine when she communicated. So, you are not voiceless trying to be this Proverbs 31 woman by any means, remember that.

> "But the fruit of the Spirit is love, joy, peace, forbearance, kindness, goodness, faithfulness, gentleness and self-control. Against such things there is no law."
>
> **GALATIANS 5:22-23 (NIV)**

WAYS TO UPHOLD HIM:

Make sure he's your first priority
Make time for him, never be too busy or occupied
Make him feel irreplaceable
Be his biggest cheerleader
Compliment him often
Always be considerate of his feelings
Let him know he is necessary
Always keep his business private
Keep eye contact when he's talking (within reason)
Try not to embarrass or laugh at him
Don't use manipulation or control
Keep from mothering him, don't nag

Don't put him in a box. He is still an individual. And his life doesn't stop because you walked in it, neither should yours. My aunt, married for 29 years until her husband died, said this when I asked her advice about marriage, "Keep it simple, don't make him your everything and don't lose yourself." Her words are very wise. Keeping it simple is always a must. Men are simple so don't think too hard or put too much weight on things. It's usually not that deep unless he is. Don't make him your everything. As stated above, he is still his own person. If he loves watching football on Sundays, it is not likely to change because you walk in. If he goes on trips with his guys, he should still go. His behavior on these trips should change if necessary but that is about it. Men need male bonding. Don't have the expectation that your presence in his life should turn everything around in favor of you and those expectations. You'll be disappointed every time. Don't lose yourself. Just like men, women need their time too. It may be time alone or with your girls but it is necessary to make sure you take care of you. Listen to your soul, your female intuition. You'll know when it's time to slow down, when it is time to rest, stop doing a bad habit, or incorporate better ones. Being in touch with yourself is a big part of being feminine and the essence of being a Proverbs 31 woman.

DOING GOOD ZONE: HOW TO DO GOOD

CREATE A JUDGE FREE ZONE. Do not judge your husband based on his past. If you have chosen him, all of him comes with the package. There are no components you can take away, alter or nip and tuck. Fully accepting him for who he is, is a major key. Be mindful of judging him for his not-too-distant past or present as well. No one wants to hear old stuff brought up in an attempt to prove a point, tear down or to be judged. This is hard because women remember everything. Dear God, help us.

Learn to forgive and move forward. Keep in mind that when someone is trying to change, it takes time. Your time may not match up with their progress. Learn to be understanding and supportive during the process of growth. Have patience and trust that he and God have it under control.

Trying journaling instead of expressing things when it's heated or you are in "your feelings." This is a way to vent if necessary so you don't sound like you're nagging or pressuring him. NO man wants to feel pressured for anything. Control your ego and emotions, remain in the judge free zone.

ASSIST. This is your husband, he needs help. And not hired help, it needs to come from you. Think of it as working as a personal assistant for a celebrity, whatever the need, you provide. Granted, most women can't wait on their husbands around the clock, but the same way a personal assistant is attentive, takes initiative and aims to please with a smile and a latte in hand, is the same way you should approach it. "What can I do for you?" "Do you need help?" These are questions to ask as a help-meet. I mean this is the love of your life, correct. Ok, then no problem. No biggie. You got it, you have what he lacks. You know him and fill the voids. You bridge the gap. You save the day. What would he do without your assistance—make him echo the sentiment.

PROVE YOUR DEVOTION. Show him. Put your money where your mouth is and show him how much you appreciate him. Gratitude is the best attitude. Show him how grateful you are to have him in your life. Try a simple public gesture like a social media post, positive character traits are a great start (you don't have to state specifics, like storytelling, etc.). It is a simple, yet public way to brag about how wonderful your husband is.

Leave him notes in random places that he'll find and smile. Send him a surprise at work. Send him a card in the mail (I know, but it's cute). Treat him to a "me" day, schedule his appointments for him, transport him so he can just relax. Think of something creative specific to his needs and liking. Pinterest has great ideas about things you can do for dates, special couple related holidays like Valentine's Day and Sweetest Day. The possibilities are endless.

KEEP IT SACRED. In order to keep it good, interference from outsiders should be minimal. And by minimal, I mean counseling only. Godly unbiased counseling. God should be the foundation and prayer, a lifestyle. Your husband should be your "go to." Be influenced by your spouse before your family and friends. Marry the right guy (If you're married to the right guy) and this will be a wonderful walk in the lavender fields of France, calming with a huge reduction in inner turmoil and stress. Keep the marriage sacred and private. All matters should be handled between the two of you. Communication is a major factor, you should marry or be married to your best friend. Making the lines of communication extremely natural at all times. Self-expression is always easy because you are open and free to be yourselves.

SLEEP WELL. Don't go to bed mad or with mixed emotions. Be quick to forgive and move forward. Make love not friction. Lots of love. Like knock you out it's so good love. This is the only person in life you've ever loved and ever will love (in this capacity, hopefully). No bad energy in the bed. Make it an agreement to not go to bed mad or irritated. And sleeping in another room is a no-no. That's a cop out. Discuss what needs to be talked about hug and make love. Sleep well.

DAY 3
Questions

| Verse 12 - "She brings him good, not harm, all the days of her life."

What stood out this chapter?

_____

_____

_____

Do you agree with the way western society has "structured" families? If not, what would you change? In your own home?

_____

_____

_____

_____

If you're not married, what ways can you foster a good family for the future?

_____

_____

_____

_____

"Know Your Position" sounds subservient, but it's not. There has to be order and in this case, the man is the head. In what ways can you make him feel like the head of the household?

_____

_____

_____

_____

By the husband knowing his position and you knowing yours, you can work together to build the kingdom. Do you think that's good? Why or why not?

_____

_____

_____

_____

How can you conduct yourself to bring your husband or future husband good?

_____

_____

_____

_____

Books:
Man Leads: Woman Follows, Everyone Wins by Ro Élori Cutno
The Art of Forgiving by Lewis B. Smedes
Picture Perfect by Lakia Brandenburg

Bonus Comments:

_____

_____

_____

_____

_____

_____

_____

_____

"
She selects wool and flax and works **with** eager hands.
"

4

BE RESOURCEFUL

| Verse 13: "She selects wool and flax and works with eager hands."

Interpretation: She is prepared and seeks out what is needed, she organizes and works with her hands. She is resourceful. She makes life easy for her husband. It is her contribution to the family.

She sews, it's one example of her hard work ethic and dedication. She finds the materials necessary to provide clothing for her family.

Materials she used back then:

Flax, a blue flowered herbaceous plant used for textile fiber from its stalks.

Wool, soft curly or wavy hair from the coat of a goat, sheep or similar animal. More than just providing clothing, this scripture symbolizes her resourcefulness to seek and find materials to use to make clothing. Umm, flax is food, like she used food fibers to make clothes. That is really impressive. Women are natural creators thus creative. That creativity gives us the natural ability to take something small and make it into something large. We take a seed and develop a baby, we make a house a home, take yarn and make clothing, need I say more? We are resourceful.

She worked to help her family. She didn't just work, she worked with her hands. She is happy to do so and it was an honor. The willingness to work with your hands says a lot about your character. One, you're not lazy. Two, you don't mind getting your hands dirty to help. Three, you're not too good to be used, spiritually symbolic of whether or not God can use you. He wants to use those who are willing to work even if it means getting your hands dirty. Keep in mind that all earthly relationships are a direct reflection of your relationship with The Father. How you manage relationships on earth are deeper than you realize. Our interactions with others are significant as well. God is testing and grooming us all the time.

I know the traditional way of working in many instances doesn't require hard labor like that anymore. However, you can be resourceful in providing for your family. Transparently, I wasn't sold on the stay at home mother stuff. I saw my mother do it early in my childhood and shortly after my folks divorced. I despised it to say the least. Like why do all of that, raise kids, go to school, be in a God-fearing home and still end up divorced. I went the other way. I worked to become independent. But now I realize my role as a woman. I realize the position I have in this world according to God. I know there are a lot of independent women that will read the pages of this book. I say to you, it's ok to be a stay at home mother. It's ok to use creative resources to provide and do your part for your family. Do it and still live in purpose. It's ok to have four-degrees and the corner office in a high-rise. Why? Because God created you for an even more important role, that of a wife and possibly a mother. To be a helper, building strong families and communities.

APPLYING: BE RESOURCEFUL.

You can be resourceful using tools such as Pinterest, YouTube and various apps, usually without even leaving your home. Learn to sew. If sewing is not an option then providing reasonable clothing is key. And let me be clear that it is more than sewing. The point is to learn to use your hands, period! God wired women to be creative. I bet if you really think about the things in your house you can come up with a way to make money. Even if you sell some of your gently used designer clothes on eBay you can make money. Do you like jewelry? Learn to make your own and sell the products on Etsy. Or instead of buying gifts, make gifts. See chapter 15 "Own Your Own Business" for more ideas.

Resourceful, having the ability to find quick and clever ways to overcome difficulties. This is what women do, it's in our DNA. Women improvise and make it work. And oftentimes without husbands knowing the magic that it took to perform the miracle. You just have to be willing to put in the work to be resourceful. Remember he trusts a P31 woman so do what you have to do to make things easy for him and the rest of the family. Do it with thought, care and pride.

> "Houses and wealth are inherited from parents, but a prudent (acting or showing care and thought for the future) wife is from the Lord."
> PROVERBS 19:14 (NIV)

Being resourceful with money is so necessary especially in the days of inflation. Find coupons or discounts, become a member of clubs like Costco, Sam's Club, AAA, etc. Also use apps like Retail Me Not, that offer discount codes to retailers across the US. Waiting until things that you need go on sale is also helpful. Like buying things off-season or at discounted stores. How about thrift stores or shopping online to cut cost? Don't forget about yard sales, better yet estate sales you'd be surprised what you can find. Be on the lookout for moving sales too. People who are moving are trying to get rid of as much as possible quickly especially those moving out of state. You can get really nice things for super cheap. Just think, the money you save can go toward vacations, college tuition or to the needy.

NOTE: Many banks, credit card companies, airlines, retailers and cell phone carriers offer cash back or reward programs. They offer discounts on purchases as well as rewards points that can help you save on the back end. Try to get the most bang for your buck. And look for specials, your favorite restaurant may offer discounts on specific days or times of day. If you are a regular customer you may find businesses that have honor programs, you know those "Buy 9 get the 10th FREE" deals. Or try Groupon it's great for all types of discounts. Take advantage of your resources.

BONUS: Corporate Discounts. There are companies out there that offer corporate discounts. This is especially true if you work at a large company. It's as easy as contacting your HR staff to see what perks are offered to you as an employee. If you work for a smaller company, consult your HR team and ask if they can work out deals with local businesses on behalf of their employees. Like gym memberships, etc. You never know, your assertiveness could save you money!

SUGGESTED WAYS TO SAVE:

Websites:
eBay www.ebay.com
Amazon www.amazon.com
Groupon www.groupon.com
Ibotta www.ibotta.com
Brad's Deals www.bradsdeals.com
Overstock www.overstock.com
Slickdeals www.slickdeals.net
Ebates www.ebates.com
Craig's List www.craigslist.com
Zulily www.zulily.com
Fingerhut www.fingerhut.com

Memberships:
Costco
Sam's Club
BJ's
AAA

Discount Stores:
Walmart
Aldi
Dollar General
Family Dollar
99 Cents Store
Ollie's Bargain Outlet

Discounted Retail Stores:
Ross Dress for Less
Marshall's
TJMaxx
Kohl's
H&M
Lulu's
SheIn

ASOS
Zara
Few Moda
Mango
Topshop
Stylekeepers
Front Row Shop
Pixie Market
& Other Stories
Wanderlust & Co (jewelry)

Thrift Stores:
Once Upon a Child
Goodwill
Salvation Army

**You can make money from trading clothes
from these companies/stores:**
Cross Roads Trading Company
Buffalo Exchange
ThredUP App
Pluto's Closet

One suggestion is to try Rent the Runway where you can rent a dress, wear it, and return it. It comes with a free backup size and free returns. Prices start at $69 and you know you can't beat that! Check out the site at: www.renttherunway.com.

It's helpful to share these kinds of good finds with each other, not just shopping but with all great things that you learn or find out about.

Have you ever been to a clothes swap? It's the best thing ever! It is a gathering where each person brings gently-used clothes, purses, jewelry and shoes that they'd like to swap or get rid of. If you have some stylish friends, this is a win. You can serve dinner or snacks, wine and cheese. Perhaps you can use this platform to introduce a new product, a new business venture or announce some exciting news. Maybe there are a small group of new mothers you can organize to exchange clothing, books and information about motherhood. The possibilities are endless and sharing is the overall theme, it's a time of sisterhood. Remember to donate the leftover items to local shelters or donation centers like Goodwill and The Salvation Army.

P.S. An old wives' tale is to freeze your sweaters to kill bad smells and bacteria.

WOMEN'S BOXES

Subscription boxes are a thing. There are tons of subscription-based boxes for items like: clothing, beauty products, books, tabletop games and more. The great thing about these boxes is that they guarantee you take care of yourself as you continue to take care of your husband and family.

BEAUTY.	CLOTHING.	BOOKS.	OTHER.
Birch Box	Stitch Fix	OwlCrate	PopSugar
Ipsy	Fabletics	Book Riot's	fabfitfun
Allure Beauty	Trunk Club	Storyed Crate	Scentbird
Play by Sephora	Golden Tote	Cozy Reader Club	Vegan Cuts
Petit Vour	Wantable Style	The Book Drop	PrettyFit
Glowing Beets	Underclub	BookCase.Club	Spicy Subscriptions
Cocotique	Tog + Porter	Novel Tea Club	CAUSEBOX
Wantable	Le Tote	The Book(ish) Box	Art in a Box
	The Real Real		Ivory Clasp
	Nuuly		Rocks box
	Box of Style		Winc

BONUS: Crate Joy has tons of boxed subscriptions to choose from. Box subscriptions for flowers, babies, books, jewelry, wine, planning, art supplies and the list goes on. Visit: www.cratejoy.com.

DIY Websites:
Pinterest www.pinterest.com
eHow www.ehow.com
Youtube www.YouTube.com
Better Homes & Gardens www.bhg.com/decorating/do-it-yourself/
Do It Yourself www.DoItYourself.com

DIY Network www.diynetwork.com
Instructables www.instructables.com
Craftster www.craftster.org/
Green Up Grader www.greenupgrader.com
Make www.makezine.com

Coupon: Websites
Coupons: www.coupons.com
Redplum: www.redplum.com
Smartsource: www.smartsourcecoupons.com
Target Coupons: http://coupons.target.com
Kroger: www.kroger.com/coupons
Hopster: www.hopster.com
Flipp: www.flipp.com
Common Kindness: www.commonkindness.com
Mambo Sprouts (Organic): www.mambosprouts.com/coupon-gallery
Whole Foods: www.wholefoodsmarket.com/Coupons
Betty Crocker: www.bettycrocker.com/coupons
Pillsbury: www.pillsbury.com/coupons
Johnson & Johnson Healthy Essentials: www.healthyessentials.com
Earth Fare Coupons (Healthy): www.earthfare.com/weeklyflyer
Tablespoon: www.tablespoon.com/coupons
Saving Star: www.savingstar.com
P&G Everyday: www.pgeveryday.com/tag/printable-coupons
Tylenol Coupons: www.tylenol.com/coupons

Apps:
Retail Me Not (Restaurants too)
Rakuten (Shopping that pays you back on your favorite stores)
SnipSnap (Retail)
Hand-Picked ScoutMob (Available in most major cities)
GasBuddy
GoodRX (Prescriptions)
Walmart Savings Catcher
Target Cartwheel
Swap
Ibotta (Rebate)

Ebates (Rebate)
Checkout 51(Rebate)
GroceryIQ
Honey
Shopkick
Coupons.com
ShopSavvy
SavingStar

SUGGESTED FOOD VIDEOS TO WATCH:

You can watch these videos to help come up with some really cool ideas for great meal plans that are fairly quick and easy. From meals, snacks and desserts the ideas are plenty. If you have a Facebook or Instagram this is how I access videos from the list below. You just type in the name in the search section and the pages will pop up. Look for their videos and enjoy. It's all about maximizing your time and the more time you can save on preparing meals the more time you'll have for family.

Delish: Facebook and Instagram
Bosh!: Facebook and Instagram (Bosh TV)
Tip Hero Recipes
Tasty: Facebook and Instagram (Buzz Feed Tasty)
TasteMade: Facebook and Instagram
Little Things: Food
Food Network: Facebook and Instagram
Goodful: Facebook and Instagram
Sweet Peas & Saffron: Facebook and Instagram (Sweet Peas and Saffron)
12 Tomatoes: Facebook and Instagram
So Yummy: Facebook and Instagram
Cooking Panda
BuzzFeed: Food: Facebook and Instagram
Get in my Belly
That Food Feed (Instagram only)
Incredible Recipes

If you are too busy to get to a store for groceries or if you need an easier option on any given night, order food. Skip going through the drive-thru. There are food delivery companies that will bring your favorite meal from your favorite restaurants with the easy touch of your phone. There are also weekly meal prep services that deliver a week's worth of food pre-made to you. There are even companies that provide the ingredients for you to prepare on your own. Sun Basket is one of them. It's a subscription-based company from California that ships ingredients for meals on a weekly basis. There are customizable options to include vegetarian and gluten-free dietary needs and the ingredients are certified organic. You can cancel or skip a week if necessary. And it'll save you a trip to the grocery store thus saving you time. I personally think this is a great idea if you have a business trip or girl's vacation that takes you away from home for a week. Order a week's worth of meals and make sure your family is taken care of while you're away. Genius!

SUGGESTED COMPANIES THAT DO THE SAME:
Blue Apron
Terra's Kitchen
Hello Fresh
Home Bistro
Schwan's Home Delivery
Boxed Wholesale
Gather by Ayesha Curry
Green Chef

RESTAURANT FOOD DELIVERY APPS:
Grubhub
UberEATS
Instacart
Postmates Inc.
Yelp EAT24
Doordash
Seamless
Caviar, Inc.
Delivery.com

GROCERY DELIVERY COMPANIES:

Postmates, Inc. (They deliver groceries too)
Shipt
Instacart, Inc.
Amazon Fresh
Plated
Splendid.Spoon (Plant-based meals)
Green Chef (Plant-based meals)

NOTE: Keep in mind that major cities are going to offer more of these types of conveniences. But you can check your local area for grocery store and food delivery services, you might be surprised what is available to you for a nominal fee. You can always have a responsible teen pick up things for you. I'm all for the old days of "Ask thy neighbor for a cup of sugar," and it's a way to stay connected to those in your neighborhood. Use your resources.

Have you ever considered a garden? My grandmother used to have a garden. It was a decent size and it was full of carrots, greens, tomatoes, lettuce and Lord only knows what else. I didn't get it back then but I do now. I wish tending to a garden was a skill I knew.

Writing this book, I discovered vertical gardens you can have in the home! There are a few different versions out there at Target and Wal-Mart and others that you can purchase online. The point is to grow your own plants and herbs. It's just a small way to use fresh herbs and or have living plants in the home. If you're concerned about the food you provide for your family then try growing fruits and vegetables of your own that way, you'll know they are free of chemicals. Above ground boxed gardens are becoming a thing, try one.

BENEFITS TO HAVING A GARDEN:
Chemical-free food
Fresh fruits and veggies
Saving money
Gardening is a form of exercising
It can be therapeutic
Peace of mind knowing that your food is chemically free
Helps the environment

"Growing your own food is like printing your own money."
RON FINLEY

Use natural products instead of strong chemically based ones around your home. Try to make natural soaps, deodorants, oils and moisturizers, anything that the skin will absorb. Think about it, your skin is the largest organ on your body and it is meant to protect things from entering your pores. Toxins and chemicals from products that are not natural can seep through your pores, or small openings. And with the use of pesticides and other toxic things threatening the healthiness of the food you consume, the last thing you need to do is add to the chemicals with what you put on your body. That's why it is so important to drink lots of water to help flush the bad stuff out. More on that later.

SUGGESTED NATURAL CLEANING PRODUCTS TO PURCHASE:
method
Seventh Generation
Mrs. Meyer's Clean Day
The Honest Co.
Dr. Bronner's Products
biokleen
Simple Green Naturals
Ecover
Green Works
sYoung Living Thieves Household Cleaner
Grove Collaborative
Hello Bello

Cleaning the house can be taxing and clearing out the home of necessary items like spring cleaning can make it more of a challenge. I recommend doing a detailed cleaning twice per year. Heading into fall or winter and then spring or summer. If you coordinate the cleaning with switching out your wardrobe, you'll find it a lot easier. It is the perfect time to get rid of clothes and unwanted items. When it comes to getting rid of those items you can donate them or sell them for profit.

DONATIONS.	DECLUTTER APPS.	DECLUTTER WEBSITES.
Goodwill	LetGo	Decluttr
Salvation Army	OfferUp	Amazon Seller Marketplace (App too)
Local Libraries (Books, DVDs, CDs)	5miles	Craigslist
Dress for Success	Mercari	eBay
Pickup Please	Carousell	Facebook Marketplace
eBay Giving Works	Depop	
Habitat for Humanity	Vinted	
Restore	Shpock	
Baby2Baby	Poshmark (Clothes & accessories)	

I believe that a resourceful woman thinks outside the box. She is innovative, sharp and extremely creative, it's in her DNA. Not only does she come up with ways to save she designs ways to help her husband and family navigate through life more efficiently.

Use the following detox checklist as inspiration:

DETOX CHECKLIST

BEDROOM
- Donate Rarely Used Items
- Examine Each Piece
- Condense Hangers
- Keep T-Shirts in 1 Drawer
- **Donate:**
- 1) What Does Fit
- 2) Things You Have in Excess
- 3) Clothes Out of Your Style
- 4) What You Wouldn't Purchase

KITCHEN
- Throw Out Old Spices
- Toss Stained Tupperware
- Basket for Tupperware Lids
- Toss Old Coffee Mugs
- Limit Water Bottles
- Donate Random Dishes
- Donate Rarely Used Item
- Create Space For Each Item
- Draw Dividers
- Condense Kid Dishes
- Basket for Kid Dishes
- Baskets /Labels for Pantry

BATHROOM
- Cabinet Organization (Toss Old Bottles, Make-Up, Old Hair Products, etc.)
- Medicine Cabinet
- Linen: Towels, Face Cloth, Hand Towels

HOME OFFICE
- Store Supplies
- Shred Documents
- Toss Old Pens/Calendars
- Filing (Taxes 5 Years, Medical, House, Warranties, etc.)
- Inventory/Restock Items (Paper, Printer Ink, Stamps, Pens/Pencils, etc.)
- **Organizing:** Photos, Kids Artwork, Media, Calendars

MINIMIZING
- Removing Old Items
- Bedroom _____ Total
- Bathroom _____ Total
- Kitchen
- Dining Room
- Living Room

STORAGE UNIT
- Clean-Up
- Organize
- Removal
- Moving In/Out

DAY 4
Questions

| Verse 13. "She selects wool and flax and works with eager hands."

What do you do to provide resources for your husband or family?

_____

_____

_____

If you're not married, what can you do now or what have you been doing that you believe is resourceful?

_____

_____

_____

_____

There are lots of ways to be resourceful. Name a few things not mentioned in the book?

_____

_____

_____

_____

Were you familiar with all of the resources listed? What things are you going to add in your daily life?

_____

_____

_____

Would you consider gardening?

_____

_____

_____

Are there any products you'd consider making at home now that you've read the chapter? Natural products can help in the amount of toxins you and your family are exposed to.

_____

_____

_____

Make plans to do your own clothes swap:
Date:
Time:
Guests:
Theme (Like "Spring Things"):
Product to Introduce/Share:
*Remember to donate what is not swapped or traded.

Books:

Household Wisdom: Everything You Need to Know About Making Your House a Home by Shannon Lush & Jennifer Fleming

The City Homesteader: Self-Sufficiency on Any Square Footage by Scott Meyer

The Complete Book of Clean: Tips & Techniques for Your Home by Toni Hammersley

Bonus Comments:

_____

_____

_____

_____

_____

_____

_____

_____

She is like the merchant ships, bringing **her food** from afar.

5

ANTICIPATE HIS NEEDS

Verse 14: "She is like the merchant ships, she bringing her food from afar."

Interpretation: She's resourceful, thinks ahead and is prepared. Therefore, her top priority and those she loves benefit. Merchant ships supply. They supply the demand of the area in which they serve. This noble woman is no different. If her husband and family are in need of something there is no amount of distance, she will go to make sure they have it. She goes off, a far gets what is needed and brings it back. So, she is also good with money. She is able to create goods, trade and negotiate and tough enough to make the commute to do so. She is no push-over, no door mat. She'll do what is needed to take care of her husband and family.

For the working wife: You have a purpose that God made you for. The Heavenly Father left out no detail concerning you. One universal thing you were created for is to be a wife. "Therefore, shall a man leave his father and his mother, and shall cleave unto his wife: and they shall be one flesh." Genesis 2:24 (KJV). So, before woman had duties or responsibilities, she had a God ordained role of being a wife. Don't let Western society and the laws of this land or your career position keep you from understanding that purpose. It's an all-important role that in modern times is not necessarily pushed like education and careers.

Before you are to become a mother, you should be a wife. Look, this in no way is meant to make those who had children before marriage feel bad or looked down upon. Back in the day women were groomed and taught how to take care of the home first. Not go to college and be

> "A woman is a wife before she gets married. There are women that are wives waiting. He that findeth a wife findeth a good thing. It didn't say he that findeth a woman cause every woman is not a wife and you can't make a wife out of her just because she's a woman."
>
> BISHOP T.D. JAKES

a career woman. Trust me, I have a four-year degree I'm working in my field, I love it. However, I'm writing this book in an effort to prepare for marriage at age 39. I am this woman. My role as a wife was totally on the back burner for a number of reasons. Most of which can be summed up to fear and hurt.

The bottom line is the importance of the role of being a wife. Taking the time to be a good wife, a role God created you for. Made for companionship, a help-meet, to help meet the needs of the man. To be suitable in every possible way, emotionally, physically, socially, mentally and spiritually. It might not sound good but women are created for men. But our role is all so very important and as a husband and wife team you are building strong families that positively affect your community in order to unify nations. So, taking on the role of a good wife is vital in the fabric of healthy families. You are needed and necessary even if you work full time. Just remember the all-important role you were designed for, wife. It is a top priority.

My thoughts about the average working American woman:

"She buys into the notion that her career is King and ruler in her life putting all other things aside. She is

the, American Dream. She makes her way loan by loan to afford a post-secondary education. Graduating the top of her class, Magna Cum Laude with a crap load of debt. She with the high probability for only getting a lower level job fresh out of college. She works, works hard only to be burdened down by the debt she carries from her, American Dream.

Trying to live a little realizing that will never happen unless she makes more money and the only way to make more is another degree. On to graduate school, she defers her loans. This is the only way to go it is the, American Dream.

As she nears the completion of her program, she realizes that she's aged a bit. Buying into the "it's better to own then rent" concept she purchases a home. Something to retreat to, family can visit, I can host holiday dinners in this here home during my 30-year loan. My future husband can come live with me too oh the, American Dream.

I'll decorate it and make it cozy according to my liking she imagines. Now she's got just enough to pay for it, the car, the finest clothes, shoes and bags after the job promotion. She'll go on and work like a horse, stressed out the higher up she goes. Vacations, she won't take because she'll get too far behind. She'll spend lots of nights in that big but empty home wishing that she had someone to share it with. Too busy to date living the corporate life as her "biological clock" is ticking. Her career is King and ruler in her life putting all other things aside. She is single, driven, a workaholic, shopaholic, homeowner...she is the, American Dream."

> "The most important work you will ever do will be within the wall of your own home."
> UNKNOWN

She knows her husband and his needs. She anticipates his needs. Courtesy of Paula White Covenant Living Holy Bible:

1. Sexual Fulfillment
2. Recreational Companionship
3. Attractive Spouse
4. Domestic Support
5. Admiration

APPLYING: ANTICIPATE HIS NEEDS.

Do everything to provide your husbands needs first. What does he like? Keep it spicy, bring exotic surprises, try to come up with creative things to do to meet his needs. But also, be willing to go far to find what is best and logical for him and the household. Going outside of the neighborhood or area for the best food, clothes (sales) and necessities. Figure out how to use those funds for honest profit.

Once your husband is squared away then make sure that the rest of the family is taken care of. The husband is always first. Raising a child, young children specifically this can be difficult. Training the child is key in the beginning in order to make this a reality. I have witnessed this personally. Consult your Pediatrician for instructions. Unless there are medical or mental issues putting a child on a trained schedule is possible. No entering the room without knocking, sleeping in your bed often, dictating to you when they want to eat or do activities that would otherwise interfere with the time your husband needs. Kids will run all over you if you let them. They will wear you down, figure out what works and do it over and over until you bend. Set boundaries and rules and stick to them. It will help in keeping family structure.

Let's be clear, I'm not a mother right now nor am I someone's wife. I am learning and preparing myself for these roles. However, life, research, questioning, reading and God's revelation led me here. We're all different which means we may do things differently and that's OK. I love this from Gabrielle Union: "It's OK that every parent does things differently to suit their child's needs. Every solution that works or worked for you may or may not work for me or my family or other folks. And that's absolutely OK. If someone does things differently or does not take your advice or that advice doesn't pan out the way it did for you, that is NO indication that you are wrong or a bad parent. We all figure out what works for us, our children and our families. We don't all have to match. It's ok to break from the norm and do what's healthiest and safest for your child. No one is in your house or your family but YOU. We don't all need to be clones of each other to be doing OK. The goal is for us all to have happy healthy families and that journey looks different for every family. Let's embrace that. Let's get comfortable with that. Someone doing something different than us does not make us bad people or bad parents."

> "A Domestic Goddess understands that to be effective in the home, she needs to be present in her home."
>
> **CANDICE ADEWOLE, THE BLACK GIRL'S GUIDE TO BEING BLISSFULLY FEMININE**

In order to meet your husband's needs you must know him well. Knowing him all four seasons and adapting as life changes. Does he like to do things certain times of the year? What's his favorite color, but further than that what's his favorite color to wear? Favorite color for underwear, socks, shoes? What does he like in his smoothies, coffee, what's his thing to eat or make? Does his like to take the streets or highways? Does he like long trips on the road? Is he scared to fly? My point is that you have to really know him to anticipate what he needs. Don't wait until he needs something each time, beat him to it. Don't wait until he asks.

If you have a husband that works for an annoying boss or is subjected to harsh insults to his masculinity then he needs to feel like a real man around you. You are his filling-station. When he pulls up, he's in need of something. Gas, a snack, a lottery tickets, some gum, a tick-tack, something. Be what he needs. Every man is different, every couple even more unique. You provide what he lacks. In order to meet his needs, to anticipate what he needs you have to really pay attention.

> "Both marriage and parenting are priorities. There is time and energy to do both."
>
> **DR. GARY CHAPMAN**

THINGS TO DO TO ANTICIPATE HIM:

BE HIS PEACE. A man doesn't need a strong woman in the house. He's got that under control. A completely healthy man needs a woman to be a woman, soft, gentle, warm and feminine. To be his solitude. A wife should be a refuge, your home, a retreat from the stress of the outside world. Men carry the weight of the universe on their shoulders. They have to fight battles you wouldn't believe so they don't want to "go to war" with you especially in their own home. You don't have to know everything or do everything. Outside of what you know he needs you can chill out. He'll let you know when he needs more of your help. Don't nag or pry. Let him be a man. Do what you can to uphold his manhood, more importantly be his solace.

BE READY. When you're prepared you don't have to get ready. Take the initiative. Stay one step ahead of him. Know his schedule. Most men have a regular schedule they follow. They tend not to deviate too much from their routine. Does he workout a lot, make sure he always has clean workout gear. The frequent traveler will always need miniature toiletries, fresh dry-cleaned clothes. Bonus: Shined shoes, most traveling men can get this done at the airport but having them shined before he goes to the airport is an added touch that he can appreciate. So, shine them yourself or pay someone to do it for you. Also saying goodbye and hello when he leaves and then returns is key. It should be a celebration upon his arrival, as if he's been on an extended business trip. Welcoming him with the excitement of a welcome home party. It'll make him super eager about returning.

FEED HIM. Men are always hungry. Make sure there is always something for him to eat. Cut up fruit, healthy snacks, easy ready meals, left-overs. His favorite beverages, if you know that after a long day at work he needs a stiff one, already have his favorite alcohol waiting upon his arrival. Feed him sexually too. Yes, you know I wasn't going to leave this out especially in this chapter. I mean, your groom has needs. This should be one of the most enjoyable times in marriage. It should not be done out of obligation but for pleasure and satisfaction. It is holy in marriage. And yes, it's healthy for men. You too. But why can't it be delightful for you both. Don't make excuses, stay connected especially physically. Feed him.

> "You must show & tell your man that he's the best, and you must believe it! No man can be the best in the world, instead he can be the best for you, right where you are. If you're with him, he's awesome, and it's your job as his woman to help him reach his full potential and highest level of confidence, through your support, acceptance, and lack of judgement. This is one of the most powerful ways that a real woman can love. She has the feminine power to nurture her family to all types of successes. This is the real girl power."
>
> RO ÉLORI CUTNO

R-E-S-P-E-C-T. Just a little bit. No, a lot. He needs to be respected. It's how they were created. Disrespect of any kind is a form of emasculation. Men reverence respect as love. To respect him is to love him. To show your respect for him is loving. Public display of the up most respect is like a badge of honor. It is truly putting the King in his rightful place, the top. The head honcho, the CEO, President, The Man in Charge. All men want and need to feel like they are in charge. They want to feel like they have it all under control and that they call the shots. Again, think Adam in the garden, he was in charge. He was responsible for all living things. He managed, ran everything. He was the man and nothing has changed. And a P31 woman is just fine with that. Honey run the show, that's what healthy men do. A husband connected to God will automatically garner the respect of his wife. It's up to you to always uphold it and express it with your actions and words both privately and publicly.

"Submission is a fruit. Honor is a seed." RC Blakes

BE LOYAL. Men feel like Kings when they have someone beside them that is loyal and supportive. Be trustworthy by holding the household down. The husband can function at higher levels when he knows the home is taken care of. It's the refuge and when it's out of order so is his life. It is vitally important to be trusted with the affairs of the home. It is an extension of taking care of him and keeping him a priority, which are part of the duties of a wife. But more than that the level of heart felt loyalty and support really moves men. And when you can move a man mountains can be removed. Let him know he is your King and his place on the throne is necessary. It is key to the positive function of the family.

> "Many females are too controlling, self-centered, or emotionally incapable of learning how to make a male feel good."
> KONGIT FARRELL

If you're reading this book you have a good idea of things you can do and change if necessary, in order to meet the needs of your husband and fiancé perhaps. It is important to be aware, ask questions, learn his love language and love him the way his needs to be loved. It may differ from the way you love. Read the book 5 Love Languages by Dr. Gary Chapman.

It's a great read and will help you to understand how to properly show your love toward your husband. You can also take a test online to find out what your personal love language is at www.5lovelanguages.com. I highly recommend taking the test and reading the book. In addition, sign up for the weekly newsletter for tips to expression your husbands love language. Remember, if something is wrong, correct it. If you can start doing better then don't delay.

THINGS TO HELP YOU MEET HIS NEEDS:

MEN'S BOXES:
You can order subscriptions to these monthly and bi-monthly boxes to make things easier for you and keep the hubby happy. This is anticipating his needs at its finest. Plus, you don't have to add them to your "to-do list." It's all about maximizing your time and making things as hassle free as possible.

GROOMING.	CLOTHING.	OTHER.	LIFESTYLE.
Birch Box Man	Stitch Fix Men	Man Crates	BeSpoke Post
Scentbird	Basic Man	Breo Box	Breo Box
Scent Trunk	Canary 48	Loot Crate	Robb Vices
Wet Shave Club	Trunk Club Men's	Fanchest	Watch Gang
Dollar Shave Club	Gentlesman's Box	BattlBox	Victory Box
Dollar Beard Club	SprezzaBox	Causebox	
KLUTCHclub	Society Socks	BroBox	
Harry's	Bombfell	Mistobox	
Manscaped	Menlo Club	Date Box	
Beard Care Club	Forma Supply Co.	Bookcase Club	
	JetSole	The Handy Box	

BONUS:
Date night is a must. Never stop dating. Schedule time each week. The days may vary depending on schedules but make sure that the commitment to have them is a top priority. Crated with Love is a way to make date night easier one box at a time. There are options to buy a one-time purchase box or do a monthly subscription. You can cancel at any time and they have 3-month, 6-month or year-long options available too. I think it's worth a one-time box at least, check them out: www.cratedwithlove.com.

SHARE CALENDARS:
Google Keep App
Gmail Calendar (Must email accounts have calendars)
Google Assistant
Amazon's Alexa -Echo Dot (She is a great resource especially for reminders)
Microsoft Outlook Calendar
Apple Calendar
Time Joy App
Microsoft To Do App

WAYS TO PAMPER HIM:

Scents:
Make sure the house is smelling good with candles or plug-in scents (some men are partial to outdoor smells: cedar wood, oak, bergamot, pine, sandalwood, nutmeg, vanilla). And perhaps there is a nice neutral smell you both like that will keep things fresh.

Relax:
Give him a clean warm face towel when he comes home from work. I can't remember where I read this but it's genius. It will automatically send him into relaxation. Doesn't have to be everyday but if he walks through the door or tells you it's been rough go get him a warm face cloth, have him sit in his favorite chair or lie down. Place the towel on his face and walk away to allow him to decompress. Take an extra step, massage his feet, rub his neck and shoulders. BUT DON'T TALK. LET HIM ZEN OUT.

Favorite beverage:
Always have his favorite drink around. Whatever it is. Water, coffee, a cold one, soda pop, sweet tea, lemonade, keep it around.

Massages:
Massages are a gem especially for men who are extremely physical. And men who don't have time to go get a massage. Grab some massage oil (try mixing peppermint, eucalyptus, spearmint, tea tree oils to give a

tingle sensation which will add an additional cooling feeling) and rub his feet and massage his neck and shoulders. If time permits give him a full body massage. The key to a full body massage is to loosen up the muscles, try a bath first to warm up the muscles. Using a lavender Epsom salt in the water is good. Then go to work.

Music:

I think music is a good way to anticipate his needs. Maybe he likes the oldies station on Pandora or Spotify. Maybe classical music or jazz. Music is a mood shifter. If things are tense put some tunes on and chill out.

Cook:

Men like to eat we know that. Why not cook his favorite meal without him requesting it. Again, to anticipate is to be ahead of the game. So, before he ask, do it.

Sex:

I don't know any real man that doesn't want sex and doesn't want it often. Please him. Bow down gracefully every now and again—if you know what I mean (wink, wink). Sex should not be the last thing on your "To Do List" for the day. Or as a special occasion reward gift. Every blue moon thing. STOP IT. Please him.

> "A loving doe, a graceful deer may her breasts satisfy you always, may you ever be captivated by her love."
> PROVERBS 5:19 (NIV)

REMEMBER TO KEEP IT SIMPLE. Don't over complicate things. Guys are simple. Don't think too deep. Women's brains are like spaghetti, all over the place but yet everything works even though it looks like a jumbled mess. This is why women are great at multitasking. This is how things get done. Men are super simple. I love this analogy by Mark Gungor: "Men's brains are very unique; men's brains are made up of little boxes and we have a box for everything. We got boxes everywhere, and the rule is: "the boxes don't touch." When a man discusses a particular subject, we go to that particular box, we pull that box out, we open the box, we discuss only what is in that box, alright? And then we close the box and put it away being very, very careful not to touch any other boxes." It's really that simple, one box at a time. Unless he's very detail oriented or a Virgo (very organized) he probably will go with what you choose. He'll trust your judgement especially if you really know him, and ladies you do really want to know the man you married. He will be fine with you taking the initiative to provide his needs.

Men in general are really simple. They want peace and tranquility, respect and good good loving for the most part. You are responsible for making sure those key things are a top priority when it comes to your husband. Do whatever you feel is necessary to make it happen. Take the time to think about him and his needs. Do lots of his favorite things often. Cater to him. He's your TOP priority.

DAY 5

Questions.

> Verse 14. "She is like the merchant ships, bringing her food from afar."

What nuggets did you get from this chapter?

_____

_____

_____

_____

Do you consider your husband a top priority? If not, why?

_____

_____

_____

On a scale of 1 to 10, how would you rate your awareness of your husbands needs? Not married, see further below.

_____

_____

_____

Create your own list of things you'd do to anticipate your husbands needs:

_____

_____

_____

_____

Mothers how can you balance making your husband a priority and still take care of your children? Is there anything you can remove or stop doing to make sure his needs are met?

_____

_____

_____

_____

_____

Singles:

What nuggets did you get from this chapter?

_____

_____

_____

_____

Do you understand the importance of keeping your future husband a top priority?

_____

_____

_____

In general, what are somethings you can start doing now to get in the mindset of anticipating your future husband's needs?

_____

_____

_____

Books:
The 5 Love Languages: The Secret to Love That Lasts by Gary Chapman
Laugh You Way to a Better Marriage: Unlocking the Secrets to Life, Love, and Marriage by Mark Gungor
Understanding the Purpose and Power of Woman by Dr. Myles Munroe
101 Ways to Get and Keep His Attention by Michelle McKinney Hammond
The Seven Principles for Making Marriage Work by John M. Gottman, Ph.D, and Nan Silver

Creative Books:
The Bucket List for Couples by Annette White
What I Love About You by Me by Knock Knock
Mad Libs in Love: World's Greatest Word Game by Roger Price
Good for One Mediocre Shoulder Rub: Considerate Coupons for Couples by Meera Lee Patel
Our Q&A A Day: 3-Year Journal for Two People by Potter Style

Bonus Comments:

_____

_____

_____

_____

_____

_____

_____

_____

She gets up while it is still night; she **provides food for her** family and **portions for** her female **servants.**

6

SET THE TONE

Verse 15: "She riseth also while it is yet night, and giveth meat to her household, and a portion to her maidens."

Interpretation: She gets up early to prepare things for the day for the entire household. She's an early riser. She is up before the sun rises and helps to make sure that her husband and family are taken care of. In this case she handles the family and then the maidens, young girls or women who help out in the home. Family first and then she extends assistance to those who make her family unit functionality easier. She is an extremely hard worker.

APPLYING: SET THE TONE.

You are the queen of your castle, you set the tone. You are the Queen Bee. You make sure that all of the "worker bees" are doing what needs to be done all while you are putting in work. A thriving household depends on the quality of the queen. She is busy like a bee making sure her husband and family are set.

"They want to be with a female who enriches their life and makes them feel better about who they are and who they can become."
KONGIT FARRELL

For example: it's like the day of a sports game, someone has to unlock the doors, turn on the lights, run the air conditioning, let the worker bees in, etc. All before the All-Star players arrive to perform. All before the crowd arrives to watch them win, "she, the Queen Bee" is there ready to go. It is important that the woman is a positive force in getting everyone in the house up and moving to set the tone for a great day.

Men are fairly simple. It is women that add flare to life, let's face it women can be a little extra. And because men tend to be simple it is women who really set the tone in the home. If women set the tone, women regulate the tone. Things are better if the atmosphere is inviting. Consider this, the home is the refueling station. The husband has to load up from having an empty tank. If the home is in turmoil and no gas is available then he suffers, the entire family does as well. The home allows the man to be a man. It strengthens him to be a man outside the home. It is imperative to create an environment of love and peace. You don't have to have tons of money, in fact your energy doesn't cost a thing. Light up his world. He needs fuel from you, his help-meet.

The top of the day is the perfect time to set the tone. If you get up earlier than everyone it gives you time to pray, meditate, exercise and prepare the family for their day. It sounds like a lot but even if you get up one hour earlier most if not all of the above is possible. Get up early and doing what you need to do for yourself first and then prep for your husband and family. This way you have done something for yourself before anyone else and still have the family set. I'm not saying this is easy but it's doable with structure and discipline. Your family needs a loving and nurturing touch before the day comes at them with all of its stuff. Let's face it some days are just rough and you'd love to call a timeout but try to keep pushing through. Think about how you can positively affect your family for what could be a really rough day. Know when you need a break though. There is balance and remember the help this woman received to insure the home ran smoothly. You set the tone. You want your Most Valuable Player(s) to win that day. Encourage them, love them, pray for them or pray with them and then send them off into the world with a winning attitude. You set the tone.

SETTING THE TONE:

PRAY. There is nothing like the power of prayer. You can set an atmosphere of God's presence at any moment. And praying in the morning is pretty much a necessity. Starting the day off with God is so refreshing. It's like eating your favorite desert after craving it for weeks, um um good. You can pray God's protection over your family. Dispatch angels to watch them. The way the world is now we need more prayer. And what better way than to intercede on behalf of your husband and family.

BE KIND. Being mean is not good and it's far from what a P31 woman is. It's total opposite of femininity and it's ungodly. Your husband is a gift from God. He should be treated as such. Being kind and gentle is a form of appreciation for the gift you have been granted. Furthermore, what you give out is what you'll get back in return. Be kind and kindness will chase you down.

BE INVITING. It goes along with being kind, being inviting and welcoming is a way to ease the vibe in the home. Being inviting is allowing everyone to be themselves because they don't have to walk on egg shells to please you. It can be annoying to be around a woman that is uninviting and doesn't allow you to be you, with all due respect. Being inviting is a vibration of goodness, warmth, like good music on a cool summer day. I have found that people tend to be more respectful when they can "breathe" and have the freedom to be themselves rather than accommodate someone's sensitivities and insecurities. Better yet someone who has a ton of rules that you have to follow or else the wrath of God will strike you down. Ugh, chill out. This is especially constricting for a husband. Like forcing him to wear "tighty whity's" when he prefers boxers. Let the man's balls hang. Sorry, totally not sorry.

What also comes to mind when thinking about being inviting is the warmth of an inviting home or space. And at the center of my thoughts is a Chinese concept called Feng Shui. The idea is to promote prosperity, good health, and overall well-being by considering how energy or qi (pronounced "chee") flows through a particular room, house, building or garden.

Feng Shui Tips brought to you by Necole Kane:

- Keep your entryway clutter-free, well-lit, and use an inviting aroma.
- Designate a place for guests to leave their shoes.
- Block visible access to the kitchen.
- Shut the bathroom door (and put the toilet seat down).
- Be sure the living room doesn't feel like a museum.
- The bedroom is for sleep, sex & solitude.
- Free your bedroom from electronic items like TVs, radios and alarm clocks
- Place a protector near the entryway

> "Clutter is anything unfinished, unused, unresolved or disorganized. When you create space for new things your energy and creativity will increase."
>
> UNKNOWN

MOTIVATE. Motivate, huh? I know but you are the cheerleader. Don't ever forget this all-important role. Watch cheer competitions on YouTube because you need to master it as a wife and mother. Seriously, you know your husband best. You know him on a super intimate level and you should know when he's down and needs a push. When he needs to be motivated and supported. You can motivate him and start the motion to making him better. Call it stroking the ego if you want. It's really being a cheerleader. Let your man know that he's the shit (sorry, not sorry but that word needed to go there). He's the King in your KINGdom and with him, you and God anything is possible. He is the shit. Tell him. Motivate him.

THINK. You'd be surprised as to how your thoughts manifest your reality. It starts in the mind. Your subconscious is in sync with your conscious mind and the more you ponder on a thing you attract it to you. It can affect your relationship in ways you might not even notice for a period of time. Thinking things like "He's lazy, he never helps me around the house." "He'll never change." "If I have to tell him one more time, I'm not sure what I'll do." You get the point. Instead shift your thoughts to that of positivity. That energy can create a better atmosphere, eliminate tension and emotions (energy in motion). Change those negatives thoughts even if they are facts to "He is the best husband I could ever have." "He is extremely thoughtful and selfless." "I don't have to ask and it's already done, he picks up where I need help."

Thinking in general can also be summed up to having your own mind. This woman was the complete package and she definitely used her thoughts to make sound decisions about her family, finances and home. So be smart continue to learn and grow. Read books that will expand your mind and nourish your soul.

SUGGESTED TONE TIDBITS:

- Get up early:
  Getting up earlier than everyone is a must. It allows you to set the tone for the family. Have your own time, do something you need to or enjoy for yourself. Then prepare for the family.

- Use mood shifters:
  Try music, deep breathing, or meditation to change your mood when things get stressful.

- Try a 5-Count Deep Breathing (I use this to clear my head, I like the number 5):
  o Sit or Stand. Get comfortable.
  o Close your eyes
  o Take a deep breath in through your nose for 5 counts
  o Slowly exhale that breath out of your mouth for 5 counts
  o Continue for 1-5 minutes or until your mind is clear and your mood has shifted.

- Create a quite space:
  Have a quiet place in the house that everyone can retreat to. Make sure it's comfortable and inviting. Go here to quite your mind and change your mood/tone.

- Keep electronic use to a minimum:
  Figure out a time to shut off electronics and spend time together.

Quality time can help to keep everyone connected and keep the tone in the home pleasant.

- Make themed nights to revolve around dinner:
  Let's stay Taco Tuesday is also game night or Wing Wednesday is family wisdom day where you share something new that may benefit the family. Maybe Smoothie Saturday after a morning workout.

- Pray:
  Pray when things seem to be out of hand, all the time, but especially when it gets rough. It's an awesome way to change the atmosphere and set the tone of any situation.

- Forgive:
  Always forgive and do it quickly. Don't let things pile up, forgive each offense and move forward. Remember forgiveness is for you. The other person doesn't have to know or be present in order to forgive.

These are beautiful words from Jada Pickett Smith on forgiveness: Finding our shape in forgiveness is not easy. How we forgive, and why we forgive is personal. One of my methods was humility and trusting that the Divine would give me an understanding of all my woes through the power of Divine love. What my journey has taught me is that people may fail me for whatever reason but my Higher Power NEVER does. Find your shape in forgiveness and set yourself free.

40 PROMISES FOR MARRIAGE:

Author Steve Stephens

1. Start each day with a kiss

2. Wear your wedding ring at all times

3. Date once a week

4. Accept differences

5. Be polite

6. Give gifts

7. Smile often

8. Touch

9. Give back rubs

10. Laugh together

11. Send a card for no reason

12. Do what the other person wants before he or she asks

13. Listen

14. Encourage

15. Know his or her needs

16. Fix the other person's breakfast

17. Compliment twice a day

18. Call during the day

19. Slow down

20. Hold hands

21. Cuddle

22. Ask for the other's opinion

23. Show Respect

24. Look your best

25. Celebrate birthdays in a big way

26. Apologize

27. Forgive

28. Set up a romantic getaway

29. Be positive

30. Be kind

31. Be vulnerable

32. Respond quickly to the other person's request

33. Reminisce about your favorite times together

34. Treat each other's friends and relatives with courtesy

35. Send flowers every Valentine's Day and anniversary

36. Admit when wrong

37. Be sensitive to each other's sexual desires

38. Pray for each other daily

39. Say "I love you" frequently

40. Seek outside help when needed

DAY 6
Questions.

> Verse 15. "She gets up while it is still night; she provides food for her family and portions for her female servants."

What did you get from this chapter on setting the tone?

_____

_____

_____

List a few ways you can cheer your husband/future husband on?

_____

_____

_____

Do you think you can get up a little earlier to set the tone for your home? Singles: This is something really good to get in the practice of. Start praying earlier, work out, meditate but get up a bit sooner than normal.

_____

_____

_____

_____

Jot down a few things you'd like to do to set the tone in the morning:

_____

_____

_____

Make a list of things you'd incorporate to set the tone?

_____

_____

_____

Books:
Understanding The One You Love by Steve Stephens
Courtship After Marriage by Zig Ziglar
Praying for Your Husband from Head to Toe: A Daily Guide to Scripture-Based Prayer by Sharon Jaynes
It's Complicated (But It Doesn't Have to Be) by Paul Carrick Brunson

Bonus Comments:

_____

_____

_____

_____

_____

She considers a field and buys it; **out of her earnings she plants** a vineyard.

7

KNOW WHAT'S GOING ON

> Verse 16: "She consideredeth a field, and buys it: with the fruit of her hands she planteth a vineyard."

Interpretation: Her resources create income for food or other things. She nurtures her investments and puts in the work to make sure things flourish. She considereth a field; so, she pays attention and examines before making decisions. She sticks with her decisions which are well thought out and planned. She examined, so she's done the proper research chose carefully and knows what to do with it. "With the fruit of her hands she planteth a vineyard," she multiples her investment. This is a woman that can plan, save, negotiate and make purchases on her own with her earnings! Then she manages and I'm sure yields a profit. And still makes goods or products to go far off to the merchant ships to sell or trade them.

Her husband trust her. Goodness, to be so awesome where your husband can be concerned with "matters of the court" and know that the affairs of his home are taken care of. What a relief he had. He doesn't even have to think twice about her keeping things in order. That's a huge blessing. She is wise and calculated. She does her part.

APPLYING: KNOW WHAT'S GOING ON.

You are the information channel for the family, the announcer, the communicator. That's what women do well because we have the capability and capacity to multi-task. This makes it easier to keep schedules and coordinate. And keeping a schedule of activities and dates especially if you have children is necessary. In fact, both parents should always know what everyone is doing. Your husband must always be in the loop. He may not always remember but needs to know. He is the protector of the family, if he doesn't know what's going on then you deny him of his right and duty to protect.

Not only do you know the affairs of your household you keep a close eye on what's going on around you. Your neighborhood, your zoning area, school district, city and county. You are also aware of the climate of the country and the world. You know what it means for your family. You know when prices may rise based on inflation or when things might go down, when the best time to purchase everything from gas to property. You do the necessary research, present things that need to be presented to your husband and execute the plan. Life is busy, I get it. But staying abreast on things can help you and your husband make wise decisions for the family.

THINGS TO HELP KNOW WHAT'S GOING ON:

GROUP MESSAGES. Technology is a beautiful thing. It is so true when it comes to communication. From phone group messaging to Apps like GroupMe, WhatsApp and video messaging Apps like Marco Polo or Apple's FaceTime communication is easier. You are still at the helm of disseminating information. It's important for everyone to understand the need for clear communication. Touch base if plans or things change, it is really a matter of respect for those you hold near and dear. Running late, communicate. The extra effort put into letting your husband or family know what's going on is valuable.

FAMILY SCHEDULE. You are the keeper of the household. You know what's going on with everyone, it is up to you to make sure that all lines of communication are flowing properly and that everyone is in the loop especially papa bear. Remember that the husband needs to know what's going on to help protect at any given time. So it is up to you to assist him in knowing what is going on. You can also incorporate family calendars for everyone to access. You can create a cool wall calendar with chalkboard paint, use a big frame insert a piece of cardboard and make a calendar, or use the refrigerator to create a calendar. If your family is a bit more tech savvy then try these Apps: Google Keep, Gmail Calendar and Time Joy App.

DINNER TIME. What's for dinner? Really, what are you preparing or what will you be picking up? Dinner is the best time to reconnect with each other after the day. It's a time to have conversations about what happened and what may be coming up. Today in Western society things are fast paced and most families are all over the place. That is why family dinner is so important most days of the week. Making sure that this time is sacred and respected as much as possible will create a home that is connected. There is nothing worse than being in a household of individuals that are always doing their own thing, it's like living with strangers. You may have to cut the extracurricular activities down a bit to make sure that the family unit stays strong. Dinner time is an excellent way to keep things tight. I also recommend no phones or related devises at the table. Talk. Catch up. Laugh. Reminisce. Plan. Either way make sure it's happening over dinner.

TRENDS. The only way to consider a field or property nowadays is to know what is trending, to know what's going on. Trends are not exclusive to pop culture. I'm talking market trends, buying trends, selling trends, etc. What is the purchase margin for real estate in your area, how quick are homes selling, is there a better area with cheaper property taxes and great schools, etc. Is it better to have a small business rather than a large company? If we move what is the commute time getting to and from work? Will this benefit my family in the long run? These are things you will need to consider. It is key to keep up with what is going on in your community and surrounding areas as well as the nation and world. When you know what's going on you are prepared.

EXECUTION. Not only does she consider the field but she buys it with her own money! This part is crazy to me, it proves that she was just like a modern-day entrepreneur. She earns income and with the funds she earns she is able to pitch in on invest property to further advance the family. Then she works to plant or build on the investment. See the sole purpose of her doing it was to generate revenue to help the family out. She creates the product to sell and gains a profit. Genius. And because her husband trusts her, she is able to have his back. Her time isn't wasted on things that won't benefit the family so he knows all is well in their home and "in the world." She is able to research, purchase, create and sell. Her execution is impeccable.

THERE'S AN APP FOR THAT:

Yes, there is. Having smart phones make life easier, right? I'm not sure where technology is headed though I'm paying attention to trends. Trends like the chip and pay options at the click of a button or touch of a finger. I mean you can lock your phone with your fingerprint or face recognition on iPhones. Finger prints to gain access to secured locations and on the back of driver's license. So not only are things changing, phones are leading the way. And though these phones are a big part of your daily life don't let them control it. Don't idolize your phone. Think about it, let it sink in. Please be mindful of how accessible things are and continue to be aware. Beware of how companies run their business and how regulations made by law are put in place.

And with that being said, smart phones offer a myriad of options in keeping in touch with others. When you do use them take full advantage of the good resources available. When thinking of how to know what's going on with family specifically, the APPS below can certainly help.

CURAGO: Family app used to coordinate schedules and sync to do lists

GROUP ME: Good app for group messaging.

WHATS APP: Good for when you don't have phone voice connection but have access to WIFI.

GOOGLE VOICE: An app I use for business. It's a great way to funnel calls that aren't personal or use simply as an extra number. Great if you want to screen calls too.

ZOOM: Group video conferencing website and app.

SKYPE: The original video chat site + app. You can video chat with multiple people, call them or message them.

MARCO POLO: A video messaging app.

BONUS: Try a newsletter. This is a great way to keep up with immediate and extended family like uncles, aunts and cousins. I do a monthly newsletter as a labor of love so that my family has a way to keep up with each other. It is a way to let them know of family accomplishments, announcements or general updates. The support you receive from family is a delight and a newsletter is just one way to give that support.

> "She was a beautiful dreamer. The kind of girl who kept her head in the clouds, love above the stars, and left regret beneath the earth she walked on."
>
> **R.M. DRAKE**

This chick is fantastic. It is so evident in this verse. In order to make these types of decisions there is much to consider. Her life is absent of things that are not important. Her focus, her husband, family and business. How do I use the leverage of my role as a female to make things better for the family, that is always the question. Does this serve my husband and or children? Is my purpose and God's will from my life at stake? Will this provide a lasting impact for generations to come? And then you research, purchase, create, sell and maintain.

> "We need women who are so strong they can be gentle, so educated they can be humble, so fierce they can be compassionate, so passionate they can be rational, and so disciplined they can be free."
>
> **KAVITA RAMDAS**

DAY 7
Questions

> Verse 16. "She considers a field and buys it; out of her earnings she plants a vineyard."

What did you learn from this chapter?

_____

_____

_____

What can you do to make sure you know what's going on around you?

_____

_____

_____

Make a list of resources that you currently use. Are they reliable? Is there anything you need to take off?

_____

_____

_____

_____

Does your routine serve your husband and family best? If you know more about a TV show then you do about what's going on with your husband or children make adjustments.

_____

_____

_____

_____

Single: Think about how your daily routine is. And if you can prep and make adjustments

_____

_____

_____

_____

Write down some creative ideas for dinner. Theme them out, Taco Tuesday, etc.

_____

_____

_____

_____

_____

How can you schedule things to keep everyone in the loop? Your husband should always know what's going on.

_____

_____

_____

Bonus Comments:

_____

_____

_____

_____

_____

_____

_____

"

She sets about her work vigorously; **her arms** are **strong for** her tasks.

"

8

STAY ACTIVE

Verse 17: "She sets about her work vigorously; her arms are strong for her tasks."

Interpretation: To work with vigor is to use energy and strength. She had to be strong in order to do the work at task. It took a good amount of energy every day so she needed strength.

The King James version of this verse says "she girdeth her loins with strength." *Girdeth,* secure belt or band her *loins,* lower ribs to hipbone to be able to work with freedom, hands free. She works and it strengthens her arms. The work over time makes her strong. I think this is symbolic to the supernatural strength that women have. We have the ability to bring life into this world, there is no more proof necessary.

"Do you not know that your bodies are temples of the Holy Spirit, who is in you, whom you have received from God? You are not your own; you were bought at a price. Therefore honor God with your bodies."

1 CORINTHIANS 6:19-20 (NIV)

APPLYING: STAY ACTIVE.

Health is wealth. Honor your temple. Mind, body and soul have to be nourished. Exercising on a regular basis is necessary especially in today's inactive, coach potato, TV binge watching society.

> "Health is not just about what you're eating. It is also about what you're thinking, feeling and saying."
> **LISA LEWIS**

I am under the belief that there are no excuses not to be active. You can do squats while brushing your teeth, that is at least a few reps per day. While watching TV you can rotate push-ups, sit-ups, jump jacks, lunges, squats, tricep dips, etc. during commercials. If you DVR'ed it then don't fast forward through the commercials take the time to exercise. Children, incorporate exercises by playing with them. Put a toddler on your back and do a short leg workout. Do clap push-ups, jumping jacks or run in place. This will teach them the importance of exercise and respect that mom has to get it in. What about a nice walk after dinner, a doggie walk with the kids in tow, how about walking around the track or field when they're at practice, do lunges as you wait for any and everything. I have broken down and done them while waiting in a long line at the grocery store, why not.

Start early, start routines when children are young. Habits are formed early, most of what they perceive is learned behavior. I remember my mother exercising in the house when we were younger, subconsciously that stuck with me. It is a lifestyle for me. One hour is only 4% of your day you can get away with 30-minutes of exercise per day, trust me you have time.

> "You must pay attention to your body. Try to eat well and work out as much as you can, no matter what age you are. Your body is a reflection of your soul and your sanity. It's a statement of how much in control of yourself you are. If a woman doesn't take care of her body, if she can live in a messy environment, she is not in touch with her feelings as a woman." Excerpt from Getting to "I Do"
> **BY DR. PATRICIA ALLEN & SANDRA HARMON**

Because the woman is the giver of life it is vital that you take care of yourself. Watch what you eat, think, the air you breathe, who you're around and most certainly what you do to your body. Your spirit has one home, your body is the host to your spirit. Anything that you do can and will impact you at some point. Be mindful of what you do and stay active.

TIPS TO LIVE + STAY HEALTHY:

EXERCISE. Exercising and being healthy should be a lifestyle. It is another way to display your appreciation to God for entrusting you to take care of the body in which your soul resides. This doesn't mean take care of your body more than your soul, it simply means respect it. Don't take for granted the ability to subconsciously function in full capacity on your own. Don't mistreat it by eating the wrong foods and not using it for the physical activities required to keep it properly functioning. You have to keep moving, that's the point. Exercising can be a stress reliever among other health benefits. Make it fun. But please don't leave it out.

- Exercise a minimum of 30-minutes most days of the week. Adults need at least 30 minutes of physical activity 5-6 days
- Exercise with a workout partner or someone in your family, take a walk or play together.
- Make a gym at home. Replace stair machine, use real stairs instead + can goods as weights.
- Keep moving, limit tv, computer + video games.
- Get a Fitbit or other step counters to help you stay on track with being active. There are inexpensive pedometers at Walmart so you have options. See the list of apps below.
- Park far from entrances, take the stairs instead of the elevator or escalator.
- Do stretches at your desk if you've been sitting for a while. Take a walking break around your floor to keep moving.

WORKOUTS:

LIGHT.	MODERATE.	STRENUOUS.	VERY STRENUOUS.
Cleaning the House Yoga Playing Baseball Playing Golf Gardening Pilates	Walking Briskly Rock Climbing Cycling Dancing Playing Basketball	Jogging Playing Football Swimming	Running Racquetball Skiing

EXERCISES:

LEGS.	UPPER.	BUM.	ABS.
Lunges Reverse Lunges Side Lunges Curtsy Lunges Leg Raises Calf Raises Dead Lifts	Push-Ups Shoulder Press Side Raises Tricep Extension Tricep Dips Pull-Ups Bicep Curls	Squats Jump Squats One Leg Squats Donkey Kicks Fire Hydrant Glute Kickback Bridge	Sit-Ups Crunches Plank Side Plank Heel Touches Bicycle V-Ups

BONUS: YOGA. Yoga is stretching, relaxation and meditation combined. The stretching is the biggest portion of it and the benefits are wonderful. The below are a few reasons why stretching is good.

- It increases blood flow to your muscles
- Decreases the risk of injury
- Improves activity performance
- Stretching vastly increases your overall flexibility
- It is known to help your range of motion because of improved flexibility

APPS TO USE:
Nike + Run Club
Nike + Training
Fitbit
RunKeeper
Lose It!

Aaptiv (Cost)
Peloton Cycle (Cost)
RUNNING for weight loss (Cost)

SUGGESTED FITNESS ORGANIZATIONS TO KEEP UP WITH ON INSTAGRAM:

Pretty Girls Sweat
The Girl Trek Movement
Nike Running Club
Nike Training Club
Muscle & Fitness
Fitness Magazine
Pop Sugar Fitness

SUGGESTED HEALTH + WELLNESS PEOPLE TO FOLLOW ON INSTAGRAM + TWITTER:

@likeneilarey
@massy.arias
@followthelita
@niketraining
@affordablefit
@BrittneBabe
@jillianmichaels
@fitqueenirene
@marcmadilson
@homesquats
@fitnessguru
@fithealthyworkouts
@fitness_meals
@yogaglo
@msjeanettejenkins
@herbs.health.happiness
@dherbs
@projecthealthandwellness
@TheFoodLab
@gmo_gus
@thefitinfluence

@noellebenepe
@22daysnutrition

> "Let food be thy medicine."
> **HIPPOCRATES**

EAT. There are some basic truths to eating properly. I mean the whole intention for food is nourishment, to fuel us to keep going throughout the day. I'm no expert, you can Google or log onto WebMD, better yet consult your physician for a plan to be healthy. I just follow a few basic principles…

Eat food in its raw form. NO processed food. Fruits and vegetables, protein and grains are essential. They are considered single ingredient foods. I eat anything that's going to help push the food down, so salad, grainy oatmeal or dry cereal (I don't like milk), granola, veggies + fruits. I have been following a plant-based lifestyle for a few years, I love it! I exercise pretty heavy and run around like crazy so that's proof that you don't have to consume meat to fuel your body. And there are other ways to get protein. Foods that are high in protein: lentils, hemp seed, chia seeds, pumpkin seeds, black beans, black eyed peas, chickpeas, quinoa, edamame, green peas, spinach, broccoli, artichokes, asparagus, green beans, peanut butter, almonds and oatmeal.

> "Take care of your body. It's the only place you have to live."
> **JIM ROHN**

I don't spend a lot on food either, it's just going to end up being "waste" anyway. Why waste money on waste?! Furthermore, what the food deposits and leaves in your body is very important as well. It's all about the quality of what you put in your temple. It's so very important. I love to exercise and highly stand behind making sure you are active. However, you are truly what you eat. In my case I'm a vegetable probably lettuce, kale anyone?

Again, it's about your body getting the nourishment it needs from the food more than quenching your hunger with something you crave.

UNIVERSAL HEALTHY EATING TIPS:

200mg or less of caffeine, watch your coffee + soda pop intake.

Daily Caffeine Intake: Business Insider
Starbucks Small Coffee=260 mg of caffeine, equals 1½ cups
McDonald's Coffee=Four 12 oz cups
Lattes=Five and a half 12 oz cups
5-Hour Energy=215 mg of caffeine, that's 2 bottles
Red Bull=80 mg per can, 5 cans a day
Black Tea=Six 12 oz cups
Coca-Cola=Twelve 12 oz cans per day, but that's way too much sugar.

Try coconut water or aloe vera juice. They are great alternatives to soda pops, or other juices that can be high in sugar.

Daily Sodium Intake between 1,500-2,300 mg (The American Heart Association recommends no more than 1,500 per day for most adults).

Avoid artificial sweeteners and preservatives.

Build Muscle, because muscle burns FAT!

If you're looking to lose weight, 70-80% should be focused on nutrition.

Cheat Meals 80-20 Rule, eat good 80% and give yourself a break the other 20%.

4-5 Meals a day, that's 2 small meals and 3 larger meals per day.

Drink plenty of water, your body weight is recommended. If you can't do that shoot for 64-80 ounces per day. Try to drink Ionized Alkaline Water or Alkaline Water, it is the best for you and you can find it at grocery stores like Whole Foods, Sprouts.

Try not to mix foods, like carbs and meat (especially red meat). It should be meat and vegetables. Carbs and vegetables. Otherwise the food will be in your body longer and has the potential to cause sickness and weight gain. Watch your food combinations.

Fruit, all sugary fruit should be eaten alone. Generally, as a snack and on an empty stomach.

Alcohol shuts down fat burning by 75% for 24 hours. If you know you're going to partake, drink green tea before and after to flush the toxins.

Try to limit drinking until the weekends to stay disciplined. Red wine is best.

Change Eating Habits Gradually:
Start small, once you've been successful for a week or more add another healthy habit. Don't diet, change your lifestyle it last longer. Dieting has an end date and you can't put an end date on living healthy!

Eating Plenty of Fruits + Veggies:
Try to eat five to nine servings a day. Bright, colorful fruits and veggies are rich in nutrients, eat different colors great for snacks in between meals.

Avoid Trans Fats and Saturated Fats:
Trans and saturated fats are found in margarine, fried foods, and many packaged foods, make sure you read the labels. Use oil in moderation and use olive, canola or flaxseed oil.

Eat Beans, Nuts, Fish or Lean Poultry instead of RED Meat:
Red meats contain saturated fat so get your protein from other sources and limit red meat to twice a month. You should eat two or three servings of protein per day.

Stick to Reduced Fat or Fat-Free Dairy Products:
Many sources of calcium have a high fat content so by eating two to three servings of fat-free milk, yogurt or cheese each day, you'll get the calcium and protein you need without the unwanted saturated fat.

Choose Whole, Unprocessed Grains:
Eat brown rice instead of white rice. Pick whole grain cereal instead of flaked or puffed cereal. Whole grains provide fiber, minerals and complex carbohydrates.

Sugar stores FAT. Eat fruit during the day and follow-up with water.

Eat Sugary, Salty, or High-Fat Snacks in Moderation:
ONLY if you eat good and healthy 80 percent of the time then 20-percent or the occasional treat won't hurt you, 80-20 Rule.

Use cinnamon when you can, it's great for digestion. It helps to break down food.

Meal Balance: Lean meats, healthy fats and low glycemic carbohydrates.

Lean Meats: chicken, turkey (turkey bacon and turkey sausage), pork tenderloin, sirloin and flat iron steak or burger.

Healthy Fats: macadamia nut oil, olive oil, canola oil, avocado, fish, safflower oil, peanut oil and sesame oil.

WATCH:
Sugar (all sugar)
Fat
Sodium
Soy (too much is not good for you)
Carbs (100-150 grams per day)

"Being healthy and fit isn't a fad or trend, it's a lifestyle."
UNKNOWN

ORGANIC VS CONVENTIONAL: Courtesy of EduKitchen Fitness

Organic crops must be grown in safe soil, have no modifications, and must remain separate from conventional products (the opposite of organic growing methods). Farmers are not allowed to use synthetics pesticides, bioengineered genes (GMOs), petroleum-based fertilizers, and sewage sludge-based fertilizers.

Organic livestock must have access to the outdoors and be given organic feed. They may not be given antibiotics, growth hormones, or any animal by- products.

Benefits of organic produce:
- *Organic produce contains fewer pesticides.*
- *Organic food is often fresher.*
- *Organic farming is better for the environment.*
- *Organically raised animals are NOT given antibiotics, growth hormones, or fed animal byproducts.*
- *Organic meat and milk are richer in certain nutrients (like omega-3 fatty acids)*
- *Organic food is GMO-free (Genetically Modified Organism). No pesticides.*

When you shop for produce make sure you read the labels. Produce comes with numbered labels:

Conventionally Grown is a four-digit code starting with a 3 or 4
Certified Organic is a five-digit code starting with a 9
Genetically Modified is a five-digit code starting with 8
The healthiest choice is organic as it has the least amount of chemicals.

Water, water, water, you have to drink water. The body is made up of more than 80% water. It is imperative that you drink and replenish that water in order for your body to operate properly on a consistent basis. Lack of water can lead to dehydration. And as a result of dehydration the blood thins and effects the transportation of your blood flow. Muscle tissue itself is around 75% water, to maintain muscle you have to stay super hydrated. The less water the quicker the muscle disappears and weakens. Drink lots of water!

BONUS: Drink infused water, also known as water with lemon or spa water. LOL. But drinking water with fruit is a great natural way to add a source of nutrition. Citrus will help breakdown food as it flushes your system and helps with digestion. As well as boosting your immune system by removing toxins, it is a good way to detox. I'd recommend lemon or lime but the game changer is BRAGG's Apple Cider Vinegar.

A teaspoon with water after each meal with help really breakdown your food (I try to do it at night most nights). It's super bitter but boy does it help. Note, this brand in particular is good for so many things and can be found at your local grocery store usually in the organic section.

SUGGESTED NUTRITION PEOPLE TO KEEP UP WITH:

@chocolateforbasil, Jerrelle Guy
@avantgardevegan, Gaz Oakley
@Fitmencook, Kevin Curry
@livelifeandbevegan Pauline, Health & Wellness
(www.livelifeandbevegan.com)
@thrivemakt, Health Food Store
@wholefoodsmarket, Specialty Grocery Store
@nutritionideas (recipes are in the captions)
@veganfoodspot, Vegan Food Inspiration Community
@slimboxcatering, Food & Beverage Company
Health (Facebook)
@thefoodmedic
@foodvisor (tells you the nutrition of your food)

ACCOUNTABILITY. Being responsible is a key factor to making progression with any plan. To be accountable is to accept responsibility. And having an accountability partner is a great way to stay on course when it comes to obtaining your goals. This is especially true when it comes to overall health and wellness. An accountability partner encourages you to stay in line, helping you to push through with your plan of action. I highly encourage you to get an accountability partner if you have specific wellness goals to achieve. Look for someone with professional experience like: a personal trainer, nutritionist, nurse or doctor. Try an individual that lives a healthy lifestyle, your spouse, someone who has the same goals as you do. You'll know based on the way they live if you can count on them to assist you.

> "Do not be anxious about anything, but in every situation, by prayer and petition, with thanksgiving, present your requests to God."
>
> **PHILIPPIANS 4:6 (NIV)**

STRESS. Life comes at you so fast these days and in order to keep up you need help, right? Try to remain sane and worry-free, it's never good to feel stressed or anxious. In fact, stress increases your cortisol levels, or hydrocortisone which is a steroid hormone. They are produced by the adrenal cortex in your brain and released to give you energy under stress. It also reduces immune function. So, if you are always stressed your body has a lower level of immunity to fight off sickness. It is also associated with controlling blood pressure, fat and glucose metabolism, inflammatory response and insulin release. All of which can affect your total health and wellness. Lack of sleep, bad eating habits, smoking or lots of drinking can cause high levels of cortisol as well.

The key is to be as stress-free as possible. You'll have to determine when you feel stressed and figure ways to balance it. Stress triggers can come in many different forms. Pay attention to your energy, if you are stressed then you'll feel a sense of unease at that time. The way in which you respond will keep that energy going or shift the flow. I suggest quickly finding something to be grateful for. Stuck in traffic, thank God that you have reliable transportation and don't have to depend on public transportation. The objective is to divert any bad energy to that of gratitude that way you are not increasing your stress levels.

Remember how you handle stress may be different than someone else. In other words, what makes you stress may not make another person do the same. Be mindful and empathic of others.

> "The components of anxiety, stress, fear, and anger do not exist independently of you in the world. They simply do not exist in the physical world, even though we talk about them as if they do."
> **WAYNE DYER**

SLEEP. You can't stay active if you don't rest. The average adult should be getting 7 to 9 hours of sleep. Proper sleep is needed to function but is also necessary when it comes to weight loss. Your body needs time to heal itself and that happens while you are resting.

Do away with things that disturb your sleep cycle like: cellular phones and other electronics as well as televisions. Try to calm down before you go to bed by meditating, place 2-3 drops of lavender in your palm and deeply inhale three times, try sound machines or something soothing like a tabletop fountain. What about listening to classical or spa music. Or as some people say, "read The Bible", I'm kidding. If you really want to get good sleep exercise most days of the week, it's guaranteed that you fall asleep as soon as you hit the pillow. It is extremely important that you get proper rest, do what you must without taking pills or medicine.

NOTE: Always consult your doctor before starting a new workout or nutrition regime. And these are suggestions, do YOUR OWN research, listen to your body and do what works for you.

> "Let's face it: so much of what we consume is not driven by knowledge but by basic craving and impulse. The process of what we eat starts in our heads. And no one is more in our heads than a food industry that spends billions of dollars in marketing its message in every means possible."
> CHUCK NORRIS

DAY 8
Questions

> Verse 17: "She sets about her work vigorously; her arms are strong for her tasks."

What did you learn from this chapter?

_____

_____

_____

Why do you need to gain optimal health?

_____

_____

_____

Create your own 30-day challenge once a quarter. Incorporate one type of exercise and eliminate something from your eating routine. Like: 100 abs per day and no sugar and bread for 30-days. Stretch yourself and make it fun.

_____

_____

_____

_____

EXAMPLE:

Month: June
Additional Exercise: 200 abs per day
I Will NOT Eat: Bread or carbs (pasta, potatoes, rice)

First Quarter:
Month:
Exercise:
I Will NOT Eat:

Second Quarter:
Month:
Exercise:
I Will NOT Eat:

Third Quarter:
Month:
Exercise:
I Will NOT Eat:

Fourth Quarter:
Month:
Exercise:
I Will NOT Eat:

Based on the example from p. 132 create a list of activities that you'd enjoy doing based on the exercise categories. Switch up your workout routine every 4-6 weeks.

LIGHT EXERCISES.	MODERATE EXERCISES.	VERY STRENUOUS EXERCISES.	STRENUOUS EXERCISES

What nutritional facts stood out?

_____

_____

_____

Make a list of fruits and vegetables ONLY, purchase more fruits and vegetables when you grocery shop. Be intentional about living a healthy life.

Fruits:

_____

_____

_____

Vegetables:

_____

_____

_____

Books:

Health:
Body Book by Cameron Diaz
The Vaccine Guide by Doctor Newsted
Women's Health *The Little Book of Exercise*
Nourished: A Search for Health, Happiness, and a Full Night's Sleep by Becky Johnson and Rachel Randolph

Eating Lifestyle:
The Power of Your Plate Neal Barnard
How Not to Die by Michael Greger with Gene Stone
The Unhealthy Truth by Robyn O'Brien
Meatonomic$ by David Robinson Simon
Eat by West: Simple Recipes fo Ultimate Mind-Body Balance by Jasmine Hemsley
Greenprint by Marco Borges

Cookbooks:
The VB6 Cookbook by Mark Bittman
Zero Belly Smoothies by David Zinczenko
The Paleo Solution by Robb Wolf
The Art of Eating Well by Hemsley and Hemsley
Eat Beautiful: Food and Recipes to Nourish Your Skin from the Inside Out by Wendy Rowe
Turmeric for Health: 100 Amazing and Unexpected Uses for Turmeric yyby Britt Brandon
Food for Life: Delicious & Healthy Comfort Food from My Table to Yours by Laila Ali

Vegan:
The Happy Vegan by Russell Simmons
Vegan Christmas
Apple Cider Vinegar Miracle Health System by Paul Bragg
Thug Kitchen: The Official Cookbook by Thug Kitchen LLC

Bonus Comments:

_____

_____

_____

_____

_____

_____

_____

"She sees that her trading is profitable and her lamp does not go out at night."

9

BE ACCESSIBLE

> Verse 18: "She sees that her trading is profitable and her lamp does not go out at night."

Interpretation: She is a business woman who knows how to turn a profit. She is confident in her merchandise or product. Her candle doesn't go out, she is always thinking and doing what is best for her family, she continues into the night. Always working, praying and doing for her husband and family.

APPLYING: BE ACCESSIBLE.

She is selfless. Always accessible to tend to her husband and family.

Always there to step up in case her family needs her. Her lamp is always burning. Now this sounds exhausting, I'll admit. As the saying goes "A mothers work is never done," and it isn't. A mother's work is never done because she can't quiet her brain down in most instances. Women and especially mothers are wired that way. The nurturing and motherly instincts kick in and only half sleeping is a way of life for sure. The worry is grand especially in today's climate. Being a P31 woman is not easy by any stretch but I think you are capable of being one. *Accessibility* is making yourself available. It usually just happens. Honey this, honey that or mommy this, mommy that, answer with joy. The balance is knowing when you need the time to recharge, remember this woman had help so don't be afraid to reach out to the village when you need to. Create boundaries for your husband and family to follow during your reset time, more on this in Chapter 19 "Enjoy Your Fruitfulness." Then in the event they really need you during that time you are still gladly accessible. Stick to your boundaries or you'll get lost in the mix. It may be hard to find yourself if you are lost.

WAYS TO BE ACCESSIBLE:

TIME. Make him a priority, the reality is men need time too. Don't be so consumed with what you have going on that he doesn't feel like a priority. It is your first job to make sure he is taken care of. It is a juggling act when you work full-time but it is necessary to keep a healthy family. Be available to them and make sure they know it. Try initiating, it goes a long way with men. It shows that you care and want and are willing to meet his needs.

Take "Happy wife, happy life" for instance, if the wife is happy what about the husband? If he is too busy catering to you then what about him. I personally think that saying should be thrown away. Each of you should attempt, like really make the conscious effort to please each other. Yes, there are responsibilities but to meet the other persons needs should be the goal, always. He needs you. Take the time to fill the gap in his life.

SPACE. Men need space. You'll know when he needs it, especially if he is a good communicator. Grant him the space and time. Take advantage of it and take time for yourself. This is a good time to do one of your hobbies. You should have your own thing that you do outside of him. Learn how to play tennis, it is a sport you can play as you age. I've had some older ladies kick my butt in tennis, trust me you can play. Golf is a great sport too. Try yoga, painting, pottery, read books, join a book club, volunteer, something other than bug him about his space.

ON. I think a real good wife is always on. She is always on it. You know the lamp burning stuff. With the invisible super woman cape on her back (you try to figure out how she makes it work, she just does). Each family is different and that part you'll have to figure out on your own. Always keep in mind that husband of yours is your top priority. You can't be too tired at night to turn your lamp off. Find the energy to be on for sex. I think this scripture is also talking about being available to sex. I mean night time is the right time. Let him put you to sleep. It's not like you have to do it seven days a week. Make time for it, initiate it, surprise him. Show him how much you appreciate him with a graceful bow. Always keep it ON.

APPROACHABLE. This goes with being welcoming, be warm enough to be approachable. Don't be a bully of a wife. Don't be mean. Do not be so in your feelings that you can't be approached. Your husband shouldn't have to wait for a certain time to ask you for something or to talk and for sure not for sex. He has to be comfortable to be open to you. Being open and free of judgement as well as availability is key. Embody that natural nurturing spirit. No subject should be off limits. Remain approachable and never too busy to listen or talk to your husband. He needs to be reassured that your top priority is him.

SACRIFICE. Being accessible takes a huge amount of sacrifice. It can be a bit overwhelming at times because people are pulling you in every direction. And by being accessible you forego privacy, quietness and self-care time. Your agenda and planning could possibly go straight down the drain. But it's a sacrifice you're willing to make because of your husband and family. Remember that being flexible is a gem and having a great attitude about it makes the sacrifice worth it. It is a balancing act, don't tilt too far in one direction. Remember to take advantage of the times he needs space, send the children away.

All in all, make yourself accessible. Be open to those you love specifically. Don't close them off by becoming cold and unapproachable. And certainly, don't be too busy to be there for them. I like to say, "I'm here if you need me." It's an open invitation to reach out if you need to. I'm never too busy to attend to those who need me, especially those I hold nearest and dearest. Make sure you're open and inviting. As comforting as a heated blanket on a cold winter night. Be the go-to person for questions, concerns and advice. Be a listening ear, wise counsel. Leave them better than before they came to you whether grand or the smallest of circumstances. Be easily available. Be accessible.

WAYS TO BE OPEN:

- Smile. I believe smiling is the warmest way to welcome someone into your space.

- Pay Attention. When someone is speaking give them your full attention. Face them, put down your phone or pause what you're doing. If you're right in the middle of something say, "I'm sorry can you give me a few moments?" That way you can properly stop what you were doing in order to focus on them.

- Give Good Energy. Don't act like you are bothered by interruptions, be welcoming to whatever that person wants to share. If advice is solicited, give wise information and let them know that you're here if they need you.

- Be Engaged. Laugh, be excited, shocked, amused, sad, empathetic, compassionate or whatever the conversation calls for. It helps them feel accepted and welcomed in your space.

- Desirable. And be desirable I mean likable, easy going. It's easy to for someone to approach you if they like you. When you are nice you magnetically draw people to you. In this case your hubby and family should almost be attached at the hip because they want to be near your energy.

- Compliments. Be willing to compliment, it gives good vibrations toward the other person and makes them feel good about themselves and the fact that they are in your presence. Be genuine and don't worry about repeating compliments.

DAY 9

Questions

> Verse 18. "She sees that her trading is profitable, and her lamp does not go out at night."

What did you take from chapter 9?

_____

_____

_____

What is your interruption of the verse Proverbs 31:18?

_____

_____

_____

_____

Why is it important to be accessible?

_____

_____

_____

_____

Do you consider yourself approachable? If so, how do you welcome your husband, family and people into your space?

_____

_____

_____

Come up with a few phrases to use to let people (especially those you love friends, co-workers) know you are welcoming + approachable? "I'm here if you need me." "Don't hesitate to reach out.", etc.

_____

_____

_____

Books:
How to Win Friends & Influence People by Dale Carnegie

Bonus Comments:

_____

_____

_____

_____

_____

"In her hand she holds **the distaff** and grasps the spindle **with her fingers.**"

10

DO THE WORK

| Verse 19: "In her hand she holds the distaff and grasps the spindle with her fingers."

Interpretation: She holds the distaff; a distaff is a tool used in spinning a stick (for wool) to hold bundles of fibers. She is crafty, useful with her hand, a representation of multi-tasking. She finds ways to do and be everything for her family. She can do the job even if it requires that she teaches or hires someone to do it.

APPLYING: DO THE WORK OR HIRE SOMEONE.

Work. It's that simple, you have to work. There is no getting around this one. A good wife works. She works in the home first. Her second priority is outside of the home. Be committed, a commitment means doing the work. She keeps her house in order. Thus, her husband trust her. Her husband trusts her so much that he has no need to worry about the affairs of the house. She is handling it at home and it works like a well-oiled machine.

Let's be clear this good woman had help, don't forget she had maidens. This is also a time that entire families were in close proximity making it possible for a "village" to raise the children. If you can't do all the work then find help, hire help. The teen down the street with the awesome family, hire her to babysit and pay a little extra to have her clean. Teach children how to do their part around the household at an early age. It enforces responsibility and hard work. If you have a trade that you do at home like sewing or making things teach it to your child. Whether you're cooking or cleaning, they can be your little helpers with task all around the house. I missed out on this nurturing when I was a young girl. I saw the cooking, gardening, sewing, photography, musicianship but I wasn't taught how to do any of them. I guess I didn't ask enough questions to display my interest. My parents and grands didn't initiate teaching me either and now I wish that I knew how to do all of the above. Teach even if they don't want to learn. You never know when the skill could come in handy and neither do they, children can be too young to decide learning for themselves. Skill sets are always a good idea and being versatile always helps.

> "Be the kind of woman that when your feet hit the floor each morning the devil says, oh crap she's up!"
> UNKNOWN

Don't be a woman who wants a man, that doesn't qualify you as a wife. A marriage license doesn't automatically make you a wife. It makes you a Mrs. It attaches and legally binds you to your Mr. but to be a wife is to be fully committed to your husband. Then the two of you being completely committed to God. Your marriage should be unto God, it is ministry. It should bridge gaps, mend people's lives, unite communities. It should always be a reflection of the Kingdom of God. It is your constant business to do good, do him good.

It is work to take on the role of a wife. It is not a job for the lazy. You can't expect to get hired for a job and not do the work. You can't possibly continue to not work or perform and still have a job, right? Eventually you will get fired for lack of performance. No boss or company is going to keep paying you to not deliver on what you were hired to do. The same goes for marriage. It's that simple. You can't sit back and collect a pay check for no work. At some point your boss or husband in this case will fire you. If you don't deliver your husband may hire someone else to do the job. He hired you based on your qualifications, what looked good on paper. Don't lie on your resume because you might have to prove what you put down. Understand the terms of condition. Make sure that you're a Proverbs 31 woman, that you're following God's road map for life. None of which is laziness.

WORK SMARTER:

SCHEDULE. Try to schedule certain days for designated task. Perhaps it is easier to do laundry on Saturday then Wednesday. Figure out what works. If you feel stressed or overwhelmed switch it up and try something that will release the stress and still get the work done. Having a routine helps the family know what needs to be done, when and how much time to allow things to be complete. Keep a tight schedule, if you switch it up inform the family. Consistency is key.

Remember: It's ok to ask for help. It's ok to start again. It's ok to say no. You do not have to have everything figured out.

The schedule below is an example to help you organize your cleaning schedule. For those who may not have the time or feel overwhelmed at the task, I hope this helps.

THAT + THIS
CLEANING SCHEDULE

DAILY
- Make Bed
- Tidy Up Bedroom, Living Room + Kitchen
- Clean Dishes
- Wipe Down Coffeemaker, Toaster, Table, Sink + Kitchen Counters
- Sweep Kitchen Floor
- Clean Off Bathroom Sinks + Surfaces Like Shower Wall
- Take Out Trash/Recycle

WEEKLY
- Clean Bedrooms + Common Areas
- Change Sheets/Bedding
- Vacuum Floors: Bedrooms Living Room Hallways
- Mop Floors: Kitchen Bathrooms
- Clean Mirrors
- Dust Furniture: Tables Dressers Electronics + Appliances
- Thoroughly Clean Bathrooms
- Dispose Old Food
- Clean Microwave / Toaster Oven Inside + Out
- Wipe Down Cabinets
- File Office Paperwork

MONTHLY
- Clean Out Laundry Machines, Dishwasher (Use Bleach)
- Dust: Blinds Tables Light Fixtures Ceiling Fans
- Wipe Down: Baseboards Crown Molding Vents Garbage Cans
- Clean Rugs: Bathroom + Kitchen
- Thoroughly Clean Common Areas
- Shred Old Paperwork
- Clean Garage

QUARTERLY
- Wash Comforters + Pillows
- Vacuum Mattresses
- Clean Out Couches + Chairs
- Scrub Down Refrigerator + Oven Inside + Out
- Clean Kitchen Range Hood
- Clean Out Freezer
- Detox Sink Drains + Garage Disposal
- Wash or Replace Shower Curtain
- Clean Soap Dispenser Pumps
- Clean/Pressure Wash Patio or Balconies (Furniture Included)
- Wash Windows

YEARLY
- Redecorate
- Paint: Touch-Up Rooms Hallways
- Vacuum + Shampoo Carpet
- Clean Drapes + Curtains
- Clean Throw Blankets + Pillows
- Clean Out Vents + Dryer
- Throw Away Expired Items in Pantry
- Clean Chimney + Fireplace
- Unclog Gutters
- Prepare All Paperwork for Taxes (Beginning of Year)
- Organize Closets

STRUCTURE. Having structure or organization is vital in keeping a schedule and executing a task. In order for things to run smoothly establishing order is necessary. Consistency is a major factor when it comes to structure. Make an arrangement and try to stick with it, the only exception is anything that is stressing you out. That's when it is important to make adjustments. Each family is different so it is up to you to figure out what will work. Again, if you are stressed make the changes. Cut out an extracurricular activity if it's too much.

Learn the power of NO. Don't be afraid to say NO to anything that doesn't serve your husband and family in a good and healthy way. "No, I can't make it to that meeting." "No, I can't lead this organization." "No, I cannot be in another activity." There is nothing wrong with NO, especially when saying YES will cause stress and imbalance.

MULTI-TASK. Women are so great at this. You can do multiple things at one time with ease and that's how God made us. It is much easier to get through a dreaded task when you can do something to take your mind off of it, right? Like try to do laundry while you watch your TV programs. Try working out during commercial breaks. Listen to an audio book while you clean. What about an audio book when you're sitting in traffic? Perhaps you can turn off the radio or music and brainstorm in the car for the next great idea for your business or something for your husband. Read an empowering or thought-provoking book as you wait for appointments. Hair and nail appointments usually yield down time to read, so read something good. The key is to utilize time to the fullest to take advantage of the time you have.

HIRE. If you are so busy that you can't take care of your home the way it needs by all means get help. The P31 woman had help. Your children are a good start, young daughters are perfect to help with feminine tasks. Sons with masculine chores like taking out the garbage and lawn care if necessary. They can also help with dishes. Overall children six and up should be doing tasks on a regular basis to help the household while learning responsibility. If you don't have children find one in the neighborhood, from church or an organization you're affiliated with, solicit their services for a small fee. You can teach the young how to do a trade of some sort like: organizing, filing, knitting, candle making or sewing. Hire them as your little assistant. But when you need help start with children, you can mold them and payment will be less than a professional. But make sure you take care of them and give them incentive to keep working. Don't take advantage, it's about the exchange of teaching, learning as well as getting the task done.

As for professional help, hire someone if you can't find a child to assist. Hire maid services to help clean up, there are professional organizers out there, tutors, meal planning and food delivery companies, lawn services, dog walking and more. You can drop off a bag of laundry at most dry-cleaning locations. And let's say you have to hire help to get you back on track after an insanely busy month, it's ok. Hire a maid to do a thorough cleaning once a month and then spot clean in between. Don't feel less than a super woman if you hire someone to help you.

BONUS: Try trade schools. When you need to save money try trade schools. Depending on the services you need you may find a student that needs hours to perfect their skills. Now this won't apply for everything but if you need services or something simple with low risk done for cheap, try it. Do some research and find what works for you. Perhaps you need to clear out a virus on your computer, try a tech school and see if a student can assist. It will be cheaper than calling the Geek Squad.

ENJOY. Make things that seem like work feel like fun! I think it first starts with your mindset. Taking care of the home is a privilege and an honor. It is a true labor of love. Making sure your family is taken care of should be a joy. It should not feel like an obligation. It is an honor to do for your family. And it's honorable to God. So, if things are feeling more like work and a chore, turn it around and make it fun. Turn your favorite playlist on while cleaning. Dancing and cleaning is not really cleaning. You can clean and make it a workout, killing two birds with one stone. Make dinner listening to an audio book or motivational playlist. Super tired? Try to reward yourself after doing a task. Sometimes you have to give yourself incentive. Doing the hard stuff first is best. That way it's done and the smaller things are easier to complete.

Marriage is work but that doesn't mean you can't hire help. This P31 woman did. Think smarter, use your resources. Solicit the help of little ones, your own or someone else's. If you're not good at something barter your skills in exchange for services from someone that is good at that particular task. Don't stress, hire help.

TRY THESE COMPANIES:

SERVICES.	APPS.	OTHER.
Molly Maids	Handy	Care (Childcare)
Merry Maids	Task Rabbit	Craigslist
MaidPro	Rapidfy	Angie's List
Find My Organizer	Homee	
Thumbtack		
Home Advisor		
2ULaundry		

NOTE: Check with the Better Business Bureau (BBB) to see how the company you would like to hire measures up. If it's less than stellar keep it moving to the next company.

> "Women who make a house a home make a far greater contribution to society than those who command large armies or stand at the heads of impressive corporations."
>
> GORDON B. HINCKLEY

DAY 10
Questions

> Verse 19. "In her hand she holds the distaff and grasps the spindle with her fingers."

What did you learn from this chapter?

_____

_____

_____

Do you feel guilty when you can't get around to keeping your home up?

_____

_____

_____

Have you ever hired any help? You'll find that getting help isn't as expensive as you think.

_____

_____

_____

_____

List companies in your local area that you can contact to hire for everyday task?

_____

_____

_____

_____

Write down things that your children or perhaps a child from the neighborhood can help you with?

_____

_____

_____

_____

_____

Can you think of other ways to make your load lighter?

_____

_____

_____

_____

_____

Books:
The Life-Changing Magic of Tidying Up by Marie Kondo
Organic Housekeeping by Ellen Sandbeck
The House That Cleans Itself: 8 Steps to Keep Your Home Twice as Neat in Half the Time by Mindy Starns Clark
Simply Clean: The Proven Method for Keeping Your Home Organized, Clean, and Beautiful IN JUST 10 MINUTES A DAY by Becky Rapinchuk

Bonus Comments:

_____

_____

_____

_____

_____

_____

_____

"
She opens her **arms** to the **poor and** extends **her** hands to the needy.
"

11

GIVE TO THOSE IN NEED

> Verse 20: "She opens her arms to the poor and extends her hands to the needy."

Interpretation: She extends herself to the poor and hands to the needy, she gives. She helps the less fortunate and homeless. I believe that when you open your arms it signifies being warm and welcoming.

To use your hands your offering by doing or working to help by giving time as well as material items and using resources to help those less fortunate. All in all, she is willing and makes an effort to assist the needy.

> "As you grow older, you will discover that you have two hands, one for helping yourself, and the other for helping others."
> AUDREY HEPBURN

APPLYING: GIVE TO THOSE IN NEED.

These days there are so many ways to give. Traditionally the mind thinks of those in need as people who don't have homes, food or the proper clothing. Need covers a multitude of necessities. *Need, is to require something because it is essential or very important.* Think outside of the box. Outside of the four walls of your church, temple, mosque, cathedral. Remember you can't give what you don't have, BUT you always have something to give trust me. God loves a cheerful giver.

"No one has ever become poor by giving."
ANN FRANK

You know I have found that giving in a valley or low point in your life is the best, it is double the fulfillment and triple the reward. I say reward because God sees it and a heart that is willing to give the shirt off their back, food that they were going to eat, time that they could have used getting back on track speaks silent volumes. It echoes, the vibrations send goodness back to you. But it is the heart to want to give that shines through. Make giving a priority, a necessity, like going to work, cooking dinner or cleaning the house. Volunteer and do what you can to give to those in need give NOW.

I had a group of homeless friends that lived on a broken bridge in Atlanta. I was being curious one day and stumbled on the bridge. My life was changed. I meet at least five men. They said they would rather stay on the bridge in the cold than in homeless shelters. They stated that most homeless shelters had bed bugs and being outside was the better option. I cried, my heart hurt for them. To think that being outside in the cold was a better option than the alternative of being in a warm building. I knew I couldn't completely turn their lives around but I knew I could help and I was determined to just that. I asked them what they needed and they agreed it was food. They had mattresses built as fortresses. They made fire pits for warmth. I made it back less than a handful of times with food. We talked about other solutions and sometimes if I was in the neighborhood, I'd just stop by bring some water and check on them. They were my friends. One day I went for a visit after traveling and the bridge was completely cleared out. I was devastated. I was told that the cops and city cleared out the area. I was sad for days. And each time I drive by the bridge I look, say a prayer hoping that they are all ok and God has kept them. My heart goes out to them.

What I did was from the heart, no forced effort on my end. My heart was compassionate toward them. I'm not always that way toward the needy, I'll admit. If I can easily give without feeling unsafe then I do. If my safety could be compromised I don't. At the end of the day God knows my heart. If it was up to me no one would be without food, shelter, clothing or love. I want everyone to win and be loved.

> "A kind gesture can reach a wound that only compassion can heal."
> **STEVE MARABOLI**

What I do know is that you can give LOVE for free, it doesn't cost you a thing to spread love. To exude it with very fiber of your being. To radiate light like the bright rays of the sun. It is love and compassion for human beings that surges something inside of you, a desire to help. It is that thing that pulls at your heart strings when you see or experience someone who lacks. Don't be in your bubble that you don't recognize the opportunities to extend your hand to help the needy. It is your duty as a woman to look out for others, our communities, our children, our men.

Get super creative with giving. Purchase something you need from a company that gives back. You can give to organizations whose cause you support. Donate to a Go Fund Me campaign or other crowd-fund initiatives. Invest in someone's dream. Give funds to a high school senior being raise by a single-parent that wants to go to college but needs assistance.

> "You don't have to be rich to give back and you don't have to retire to spend every day doing what you love. You can find profit, passion, and meaning all at once."
> **BLAKE MYCOSKIE, FOUNDER OF TOMS**

GIVING WAYS: GIVE NOW

Homeless Kit:
Food Baggies (Things they can eat right away, no canned goods)
Female Hygiene
Male Hygiene
Winter Necessities Package

Care Packages:
College Student
Single Parent
New Mother/Parents

Widow/Widower
Teacher

Cards:
Send homemade cards
Assisted Living Locations
Children's Hospitals (You may have to get permission to send due to medical issues)
Ronald McDonald House

Run Errands For:
Single Parent
Busy Parent
Older Adult
Disabled
Widow/Widower

Volunteer:
Food Bank
Donate Blood
Homeless Shelter
Non-Profit Walk or Run
Clean-Up the Neighborhood
Neighborhood Watch Patrol
Tutor Children for Free
Mentor Children for Free
Assist Troubled Teens

Environmental:
Limit Plastic Use (Bottles, straws, etc.)
Don't Litter
Conserve Energy
Recycle

Give To:
The Red Cross
Salvation Army

Goodwill
Church Outreach Ministries
Homeless Shelters/Pantries
Use an app (Cash App, PayPal, etc.) to donate

Create Your Own Thing:
Except donations for charity instead of gifts
Proceeds from your merchandise go toward charity
Start Your Own Charity Drives (Coat, Clothing, Food, etc.)

PURCHASE FROM COMPANIES THAT GIVE:
TOMS: Shoes, Eyewear, Coffee
Warby Parker Eyewear
Yoobi
The Company Store
Mercy Ships
Out of Print Clothing
Kiehl's
UNICEF Market
Paul Newman Salad Dressing
Global Giving
Thistle Farms
Baby Teresa
Love Goodly
WeWood
Hand in Hand
Smile Squared
Faucet Face
Parks Project
Roma Boots
Causebox
Starling Project
cuddle + kind
FEED

ORGANIZATIONS THAT FOSTER EMPOWERMENT:

NEST www.buildanest.org
KIVA www.Kiva.org
The Adventure Project www.theadventureproject.org
Fractured Atlas www.fracturedatlas.org
FEED Projects www.feedprojects.com
Purple Purse www.purplepurse.com
method www.methodhome.com
GiveDirectly www.givedirectly.org
TerraCycle www.terracycle.com
Design Dua Innovative Crafts www.DesignDua.com
Pencils of Promise www.pencilsofpromise.org

BONUS: If you are looking for charities to give to check out Charity Navigator. They breakdown organizations by category to help you determine what you'd like to give your time or money toward. They have featured organizations, a rating system and causes around the world. Visit www.charitynavigator.org.

Keep in mind that there are always going to be organizations, companies, schools or groups that need help. Take the initiative and ask. Do some research and find a local group near you. Perhaps a friend or family member is going through a rough patch, help them. You can always clean up in your surrounding area. If something bothers you it means it requires your attention. Do something about it, figure out what is necessary to make a change. Use your hands to create a better place. Involve friends, create a movement and heal the world. Use your imagination, it shows God your effort and dedication to help those who need it. Always remember you can't beat God giving.

> "My wish for you is that you continue. Continue to be who you are, to astonish a mean world with your acts of kindness."
>
> DR. MAYA ANGELOU

DAY 11
Questions

| Verse 20. "She opens her arms to the poor and extends her hands to the needy."

What did you think about this chapter on giving to those in need?

_____

_____

_____

_____

_____

_____

How will you incorporate giving in your life now?

_____

_____

_____

_____

_____

_____

Challenge yourself, try a 10-day challenge and do one thing a day to help someone else. Be intentional, pay it forward, donate funds, write a review for a business owner, a letter of recommendation, support someone at their cause or event. What about liking, following, sharing, re-tweeting someone's business you admire. Take it a step further and do the challenge each quarter. Get in the habit of giving.

_____

_____

_____

When will you commit to starting your 10-day challenge? Hold yourself to the commitment and be intentional. Try journaling during this experience, it will give you additional insight on what it means to serve with intention.

_____

_____

_____

Books:
Start Something That Matters by Blake Mycoskie
The Power of One by Steve Maraboli

Bonus Comments:

_____

_____

_____

When it snows, she has no fear for her household; for all of **them are clothed in** scarlet.

12

BE PREPARED

Verse 21: "When it snows, she has no fear for her household; for all of them are clothed in scarlet."

Interpretation: Not afraid of the snow, she is not afraid of the future or seasons to come. The house is clothed with scarlet so she doesn't fear cold or any storms. She is prepared and because of her preparation her family has the proper clothing and protection.

Red scarlet, symbolizes courage, passion, force and heat. Scarlet retains heat and was made of wool. She has no fear of their health, their wellbeing or ability to sustain any circumstance. When the cold comes, she is totally prepared. She is so ready for it she laughs at the thought of being ill prepared. She is a soldier. A fearless Queen that knows no lack because she's done all she can to make sure her household is good. She trust God.

"It's better to be prepared for an opportunity and not have one than to have an opportunity and not be prepared."
WHITNEY M. YOUNG

APPLYING: BE PREPARED.

You don't have to get ready when you're prepared. And you never want to get caught unprepared especially in the case of an emergency. Ladies is it is your duty to have the house in order. It is your job to make sure that things are moving like clockwork inside those four walls. Now the husband is the head of the household but it is up to women to keep in running.

> "By failing to prepare you are preparing to fail."
> BENJAMIN FRANKLIN

It relates to other things as well. The husband is like the Director and you the Assistant Director. You work well as a team but he makes the final call. There are details a man may leave out or forget, that is exactly where you come in. You are the multi-tasking Queen and juggling is your finest trait. You know what he has going on as well as the rest of the family so you can execute the plan. This means you are prepared.

You have the wet-ones, lotion, band-aids, tissue, extra earring back, snacks, drinks, change of clothes, mints, gum, you name it it is probably in your bag or car. Knowing what to do if someone is choking, badly cut, making sure your family has enough food and water stored up in case of inclement weather or a natural disaster. That is what women do, they prepare. And stay prepared.

Emergency Preparedness:

It is so important to know what to do in case of emergency. The family unit should come up with a plan in the case of an emergency. Have disaster plans set, emergency numbers, location to meet, bug out bags, emergency cash, canned goods and plenty of water, the list goes on.

Take the horrific day of 9/11, there was no cell phone service available for hours. I remember calling a few loved ones to check on their status, busy. Think of what would happen if there was a black out for days, no electricity. Think about how much of what you do runs on electricity. Garage door openers, gates, anything you have a card for. What is a bank card if you can't get money out? Having emergency cash stashed is important. You must not think tragedy won't happen because it could, God forbid. You need to be prepared either way. I have a really good friend that has gallons and gallons of water, canned food, a generator, bug out bag, flash lights, candles, batteries, battery operated clocks, a radio and other items. It may seem a bit overboard but she is prepared, just in case.

The American Red Cross is a great resource to prepare you. They have apps, yes apps, mobile apps for First Aid, Pet First Aid and Blood

Donation. They also offer classes, it's a great way to learn first aid, CPR, babysitting and childcare, swimming and water safety, lifeguarding, EMT and more. When it comes to preparation and training in the area of safety The American Red Cross has you covered. Accidents are one of the leading causes of death among persons from 1 to 38 years old, according to the American Red Cross. This is the case because people generally don't know what to do before medical care arrives. As a P31 woman you should at least know the basics.

Let's talk Survival Boxes. Yes, they exist and I love it. You want your family to keep going as best as possible in the unfortunate event of a disaster. You never know what the future holds but you can always be prepared. And because women are detail oriented there is nothing left out. These survival boxes are monthly subscriptions and quite frankly, genius. You can get survival food, seeds, gear and water each month. Boxes contain 25-year storable food, think astronaut food. You can cancel at any time. Visit: www.survivalboxes.com. Judy Kit is new on the scene with similar emergency preparedness offerings www.judy.co, thank me later.

EMERGENCY KIT CHECKLIST

Water: As much as you can carry, extra portable water (3-5 gallons) for sanitation + drinking, water purification methods

Food: 72-hour supply, can opener

Warmth + Shelter: windproof/waterproof clothing for warmth, Strike anywhere matches; second method to start a fire, Tent/Shelter/Plastic Sheeting, Wool-blend Blanket/Sleeping Bag, Emergency Reflective Bag/Blanket, Hand + Body Warm Packs, Poncho, Lightweight Stove + Fuel

Tools: pocket knife/pliers, shovel, hatchet/axe, sewing kit, 50-foot nylon rope, duct tape

First Aid: first-aid kit + supplies, burn gel + dressings, bottle of potassium, iodide tablets, N95 respirator mask

Communication Devices: NOAA weather radio with batteries, with alternate power sources, whistle with neck cord

Personal + Sanitation: toilet paper, tissues, toothbrush + paste, hand sanitizer/soap, sanitary napkins, comb, razor, moist towelettes, garbage bags, cellphone + charger, hand-crank or external battery

---

Extra Clothing: A complete outfit of appropriate clothing for each family member, extra socks, underwear, hat, sturdy shoes + gloves

Money: at least $20 in cash with some in coins, at least a half-tank of gas in car

Stress Relievers: games, books, hard candy, inspirational reading; for children: small toys, paper + pen, favorite security items

Light Sources: flashlight with extra batteries, candle, light-sticks, headlamp/headlight

---

Portable Container: durable water-resistant duffel bag or frame pack

Important Papers: copies of documents important to your family (birth certificates, marriage license, wills, bank info, insurance forms), phone numbers, cc information

Additional Items: extra food, camp stove, mess kits and other cooking equipment, sun block, insect repellent, portable toilet snake bit kit, special medication/vitamins or other needs, local map, compass, watch, glasses, infant needs, pet food/water, first-aid book, emergency reference material

---

The list above is brought to you by your friends at Emergency Essentials. See their website below along with other sites to help you prepare for emergencies of all kinds. In the meantime, the following are important things to know.

IMPORTANT TO KNOW

Your kit should be in a portable container located near an exit of your house. This is so you can grab it on your way out of the house in a serious emergency. Do not overload your kit-you may have to carry it long distances to reach safety or shelter.

Each family member should have their own kit with food, clothing and water. Distribute heavy items between kits.

Enclose the extra clothing, matches, personal documents, and other items damageable by smoke or water in plastic to protect them. If it's raining when you have to evacuate, you will appreciate the dry clothes.

Keep a light source in the top of your kit, so you can find it quickly in the dark.

Personalize your kit. Make sure you fill the needs of each family member.

Inspect your kit at least twice a year. Rotate food and water. Check your children's clothing for proper fit. Adjust clothing for winter or summer needs. Check expiration dates of batteries, light sticks, warm packs food and water.

Consider the needs of elderly people as well as those with handicaps or other special needs. For example; for babies, store diapers, washcloth, ointment, bottles and pacifiers, and other special supplies.

WEBSITES TO HELP YOU PREPARE:
www.realworldsurvivor.com
www.personaldefenseworld.com

THINGS TO KNOW FOR EMERGENCIES:
CPR/AED
Evaluation Plan (multiple routes out of town to include a meet up location in addition to the home)
How To Read a Compass
How To Read a Map
Start a Fire
How To Fish
How To Shoot a Gun

WEBSITES FOR EMERGENCIES:
www.fema.gov
www.ready.gov
www.beprepared.com (Emergency Essentials)
www.redcross.org
www.hhs.gov/disasters

BONUS: goTenna, is new technology using low-watt VHF waves to send text messages void of WIFI or cellular service. It's a walkie talkie gadget of sorts ranging from a half-mile to 25-miles. It connects via Bluetooth using an iOS or Android app, they are sold in pairs and come with downloadable maps as well as the ability to receive and transmit GPS locations. It has a rechargeable battery. It can be used for any remote place where cell phone service doesn't exist. Check it out at: www.gotenna.com.

BE PREPARED:

Preparedness, readiness; organized; arrange by systematic planning and united effort.

FEARLESS. I mean the characteristics of this woman described in verse 21 is what you should possess. She is resilient. She has no fear of things that may happen. Her confidence is top notch but she doesn't negate the fact that God is her strength and refuge. It is through him that she is able to walk with confidence and not fear. She knows that fear is non-existent. That it is based on emotions of something that has not happened. She knows that she's covered and having fear is merely a waste of time. You can be just like this. Put your total trust in God and this becomes second nature. Have confidence, be fearless.

OBSERVANT. In order to know what is needed you have to be observant. Watching and keeping a constant eye out for what is missing, running low, even the energy around you. This is also a part of the female intuition. That undeniable gut feeling that something is off or you need to pay close attention to a thing. Watch, pay attention, lurk if you have to but trust your gut, your female intuition. Observe everything.

SELECTIVE. In order to be good, you have to be selective. A queen wouldn't choose silk for the winter, right? Nor would she pick any material or resources that wouldn't benefit her king or kingdom. Just anything won't do for her. Be choosy in a good way, the master of quality control. And that applies to every area of your life. Select with careful thought, analyzing each detail, confidently mapping out what will work best.

PLANNER. The ultimate planner. Want to know what is going on and the next steps, people ask you. You are a walking dictionary. A resource guide. If you don't know you find out in a hurry and get back. Be in the know and have it no other way. You are the quintessential nurturer and because you plan you are able to give the necessary attention to help develop and further your husband along as well as the rest of the family. The planning you do makes it easier to navigate and juggle what is necessary to accomplish.

ORGANIZE. Everything is done is decency and order. "Let all things be done decently and in order." 1 Corinthians 14:40 (KJV). To be a good woman described in Proverbs 31 order is a brick to build on the foundation of God. So, one, without question this woman's foundation in rooted in God. Secondly, she builds using bricks. Chaos and confusion dare not step foot in her household.

Being centered with God and connected with your husband are necessities to maintaining organization. You know it and work it so well it may go unnoticed. You are the thread that keeps things together. If not for your organization it would be an impossible feat.

> "Expect the best. Prepare for the worst. Capitalize on what comes."
>
> ZIG ZIGLAR

DAY 12
Questions

> Verse 21. "When it snows, she has no fear for her household; for all of them are clothed in scarlet."

What did you learn?

_____

_____

_____

As a woman what can you do on a daily basis to stay prepared?

_____

_____

_____

_____

As a single woman what can you do to stay connected to friends and family to be prepared?

_____

_____

_____

_____

What ways can you better prepare your family?

_____

_____

_____

_____

_____

Make a list of things you already have in your home that you can use in the case of an emergency:

_____

_____

_____

_____

What do you need to survive? Write a list of stuff you need to have for an emergency of any kind based on the information in the book:

_____

_____

_____

_____

Create a document that has a list of phone numbers, addresses and other important information. Everyone in the family should have the same list easily accessible. The American Red Cross has a downloadable and print-friendly emergency contact card template. To access, visit: www.redcross.org/prepare/location/home-family/informed. (A visual example is on page 319)

In the event of a disaster, what are the escape routes leaving your home?

_____

_____

_____

Where is the meet up location if the family is not at home?

_____

_____

_____

_____

If there is an area evacuation, where would your family meet outside of your neighborhood?

_____

_____

_____

_____

Come up with a plan that the entire family knows. Run a drill to test it out, it's better to be prepared.

_____

_____

_____

_____

Books:
Emergency: This Book Will Save Your Life by Neil Strauss
Emergency Food Storage & Survival Handbook by Peggy Layton
Emergency Medicine Secrets: Sixth Edition by Vincent J. Markovchick, Peter T. Pons, Katherine M. Bakes and Jennie A. Buchanan
Spy Secrets That Can Save Your Life by Jason Hanson

Bonus Comments:

_____

_____

_____

_____

_____

_____

_____

"

She makes coverings for her bed; she is clothed in fine linen **and purple**.

"

13

BE A QUEEN

Verse 22: "She makes coverings for her bed; she is clothed in fine linen and purple."

Interpretation: She makes coverings for her bed. Tapestry in those times was thick and usually has some type of design on it. It is used for covering furniture or hanging on the walls. Let's talk briefly about the intricate weaving that is takes to make tapestry. It is much thicker than regular fabric, definitely thicker than that of silk or linen. Not only was it put together by clever weaving but with design using color and it could also include forms of pictorial embroidery. They were decorated to enhance the home and because it was thick it was made to last. All in all, she was responsible for making sure the home was warm and inviting.

Wow, that is amazing to me. The creativity of a woman that is willing to tap into her initiate ability to create. And the patience it must have took to make such a thing. Think about tribes and villages, women sitting out and hand weaving baskets and the like. They learn and then pass that along to their daughters. In turn these baskets can be taken a far off to the merchant ships and be sold or traded. What a woman.

Her clothing is silk and purple. Purple symbolizes royalty. Silk is a fine fabric usually brought from Phoenician cities, it was the most-costly of goods and highly esteemed. This outward description of her clothes symbolizes that of wealth. She was a woman that represented royalty and wore clothing suitable for a Queen. She also made sure her family was clothed with the best there was to offer because that's what Queens do.

APPLYING: BE A QUEEN.

"Love yourself first and everything else falls in line. You really have to love yourself to get anything done in this world."
LUCILLE BALL

"Your royal highness," Your majesty," you are royalty. This is what this woman exemplifies, royalty. She is a queen. She is the example of how all women should conduct themselves. She the epitome of a helpmeet. She is the representation of God's true intention for woman.

I love this description of a Queen by Author Jay Barnett from *Letters to a Young Queen*, "What is a Queen? A Queen is a ruler and monarch with the power to make all the decisions in her kingdom, which can be shared with her King. Every person has the capability to rule over a kingdom with his or her family. A Kingdom consists of your mind, body and soul. As a ruler, you possess the power to make all decisions in your life. Knowing that you are a Queen changes the dynamics of how you rule your kingdom." He does an excellent job of illustrating the role and characteristics of a Queen, so good I had to share. To help you remember who you are he created an acronym for QUEEN:

Q-quality you are priceless
U-unique there will never be another you
E-educate yourself to empower you to be at your best
E-etiquette conduct yourself as royalty
N-never remove your crown

Western society is far removed of the concept of Queen. Queen Elizabeth II is the most recent and popular example of such power in this lifetime. In writing this chapter I asked myself, what does it mean to be a Queen? How do you carry yourself? How do you speak? What decisions do you make? How do you treat others? I believe a Proverbs 31 woman is a Queen. Let's start there. She is a Queen because she serves the one on the throne. First her Heavenly Father and then her earthly King, her husband. By mere role and execution, she is a Queen. She knows her role, she takes her position and executes her job.

"A queen on her throne is a woman who has mastered herself. She's not perfect, but she is complete. She has come to the full realization that everything she needs to fulfill her mission can be found within. She's uncovered her powers and she knows how to use them. She's no longer on the path, she has become the path."

UNKNOWN

Does she walk a certain a way? Yes, with dignity and pride because she knows who she is and to whom she belongs. Does she speak a certain a way? Yes, with grace, class and gentleness. She is far removed from belittling, backbiting, condescending and self-righteous comments and conversation. Does she work? Yes, she is willing to do the necessary work to take care of her King and family. This includes delegating work or hiring help to execute what needs to be done and assisting those less fortunate. Does she make decisions? Yes, she knows what needs to be done. Her King trust her and she knows when she needs to consult him in making decisions outside of her realm or role. She is a praying Queen so she consults the Heavenly Father above all. How does she treat others? She treats others with respect, love and kindness. Her compassion and need for understanding override any preconceived judgements. She has the heart of God and she walks, talks, works and reflects his light. She is a Queen.

"But ye are a chosen generation, a royal priesthood, an holy nation, a peculiar people; that ye should shew forth the praises of him who hath called you out of darkness into his marvelous light."

1ST PETER 2:9 (KJV)

ROYAL BEHAVIOR:

I'll breakdown Jay's Acronym a little future with my interpretation.

QUEEN: QUALITY. Know your worth. You are priceless, far above rubies. It is important for you to know your value. This virtuous woman was held in high esteem. You are the best of the best, elite, super VIP. Because you are cut from a different cloth you conduct yourself differently, like high quality. This doesn't mean that you think that you're better than anyone it is simply that the standard in which you operate is high. You don't go or do just anything, you don't follow the crowd, you are a trendsetter in your own right. Others admire and look up to you. You are precise in your actions and do what will benefit your Heavenly Father and King.

> "Do not give dogs what is scared; do not throw your pearls to pigs. If you do, they may trample them under their feet, and turn and tear you to pieces."
> MATTHEW 7:6 (NIV)

QUEEN: UNIQUE. You are fearfully and wonderfully made. "For you created my inmost being; you knit me together in my mother's womb. I praise you because I am fearfully and wonderfully made; your works are wonderful; I know that full well." Psalms 139: 13-14 (NIV). God got rid of the mold when he made you. There is no one like you, past, present or in the future. You are truly one of a kind. The uniqueness that you hold is what makes you, you. God crafted you with special care to carry out a purpose. He thought enough of you to make you like no other. There is something so divinely special about you. It's up to you to embrace it, cultivate it and live it. It's specifically unique and so are you.

QUEEN: EDUCATE. Continue to learn as much as you can. Books are an excellent place to start. Keep in mind a P31 woman educates herself on things that will benefit the family. Educate yourself on things that you may need in the future. "She considers a field and buys it; out of her earnings she plants a vineyard." Proverbs 31:16 (NIV). Learn and then pass the information on to others, your family first. Be intelligent and wise, take everything to God in prayer and be led by him. And of course, your King is aligned with the Heavenly Father. So, when you need to act you are in sync with him through your divine connection.

> "Think like a queen. A queen is not afraid to fail."
> OPRAH WINFREY

QUEEN: ETIQUETTE. A queen must conduct herself as a queen. Properly greeting and acknowledging others. Treating people with kindness. Smiling, being polite, feminine, graceful and classy. Knowing what to do no matter what environment you are in, dressing appropriately for the occasion always exhibiting grace and class.

ETIQUETTE TIPS:

- Cross your legs especially in the presence of a man. At least a part of your legs should be touching at all times. Cross them at the ankles or at the knee but legs should be touching.

- Don't plop. When sitting down imagine being in a dress each time. Sit side ways and turn into your seat. Sit and slide, don't plop. I do this even when I get in the car. I have leather seats so it's easy. Just remember not to plop or flop that's what guys do.

- Make sure that you only put a small portion of food in your mouth when you're eating. Though chewing with your mouth closed always applies, if you have to answer someone with a quick response your food isn't shown or heard. Eating a small portion allows for a polite, clear yet quick response without being rude.

- Please and Thank You. Make request that include "Please" and "Thank You." Instead of yes, say yes please. Thank you is a great way to show your appreciation, it never gets old. Use them both and often.

- Always RSVP. Especially if you're requested to do so. The host needs a head count to make sure that there is room and food for you. If you know you can't go send it right away. If undecided double check the deadline to let them know. Those who invite you to join them like you and would enjoy your presence so show appreciation for the gesture and respond. I like to include "Thanks for thinking of me" when responding to any invite formal or informal. People don't have to include you.

- Ask about guests. If you're invited somewhere ask if you can bring someone. Don't assume that it's ok. The host may have something planned for you only. And you and your uninvited guest may throw things off.

- Never go to a party empty handed. No matter the location bring something. A card, flowers or a plant, a balloon, candy, gift card, a bottle of wine, something to show your appreciation for the invite and consideration. If you make or sell goods, create something and bring it as a gift. Candles, coasters, key chains, gift baskets, etc. (See chapter 15 for more ideas) bring it. It's a great way to help promote your craft too. I also believe this applies to any setting or gathering including BBQ's, Watch Nights (Boxing, Super Bowl, UFC Fights, Award Shows, etc.), board game or themed gatherings that aren't quite a party, bring something other than your charm and good looks. It's polite.

- No elbows on the table.

- Stand up when meeting someone. When being introduced to someone and you are sitting down, stand up to greet them. It's respectful.

- Acknowledgment. Don't be rude and walk into a room without greeting everyone. It doesn't have to be one-on-one, say hi to the room or group of people you have just walk up to. I use a 180-degree wave or a full spin around, a smile and eye contact work for me all the time. It's respectful to acknowledge someone's presence even if you don't care for them. Stay out of your feelings and say hello.

- Respect. Show respect at all times but especially when you're at someone's home. Follow their rules. If they do something a certain way so do you. It's their place, respect it. It's only polite.

- Cover your mouth when you yawn. Try not to open your mouth so wide people can see your tongue + tonsils. And loose the sound effects + unnecessary noise. We get it, you're sleepy and your body is telling you and everyone else.

- Use the phrase "Excuse Me." If you don't hear someone, need to interject, passing in front or bump into someone. If you let a burp (or gas, oops) out on accident...say "Excuse Me" and try remove yourself from the room if you can before it slips out. When you reach over someone, put any body part in front of their face or their body, say "Excuse Me." Getting a stranger's attention, "Excuse Me." Say it with a smile, "Excuse Me."

- Use sir and ma'am always. Those in authority should always be saluted with a sir or ma'am as a form of respect and older adults are no different. I use it to address younger people too. It makes them feel proud and shows them respect they might not otherwise get. You'll find that they will return the respect.

- Cell phones. Try to keep conversations in public to a minimum and talk to the person on the phone not everyone in the area. Wear earphones and if you don't have noise cancelling headphones then keep your music at a level only you can hear. If you take them out and you can hear the music loud and clear I guarantee others can too. When you're checking out get off the phone or place the person on hold. It's rude to talk during checkout or at any counter. Don't bring phones to eat. Enjoy each other's company. I know it's hard to resist but if you turn it off, you'll never know you have a message. I get that you may even have to show someone something your phone, I say hold off until after you eat. Most meals are 10-30 minutes long, it can wait.

- Watch your mouth. Don't cuss. It's not ladylike. If you must don't make sentences out of them and I know we all have our moments but don't cuss folks out.

- Write. Handwritten notes, letters and cards go a long way. It's extremely thoughtful and polite.

QUEEN: NEVER. Always remember that you are a Queen. It's a code of conduct. A badge of honor. Your crown must always stay on you head. Hold your head up high. Stand with humility and grace. You must always keep the invisible crown on your head. If you tilt your head your crown may fall, so head up, stay focused and walk the straight and narrow path. Remember that you represent your King and the KING of KINGS. Crown.

> "I know I have the body of a weak and feeble woman, but I have the heart and stomach of a King!"
>
> QUEEN ELIZABETH I

DAY 13
Questions

> Verse 22. "She makes coverings for her bed; she is clothed in fine linen and purple."

What did you learn from this chapter on being a Queen?

_____

_____

_____

What is your definition of a Queen?

_____

_____

_____

_____

What do you consider royalty?

_____

_____

_____

_____

In what ways can you exhibit the qualities of a Queen?

_____

_____

_____

_____

_____

Make a list of etiquette tips you want to incorporate in your life:

_____

_____

_____

_____

How can you utilize what you learned to teach a young lady about being a Queen?

_____

_____

_____

_____

Using the acronym QUEEN come up with your own way to remember to always be a Queen.

Q

U

E

E

N

Books:

Letters to a Young Queen by King Jay Barnett

It's Good to Be Queen: Becoming as Bold, Gracious, and Wise at the Queen of Sheba by Liz Curtis Higgs

Bonus Comments:

_____

_____

_____

_____

_____

_____

_____

Her husband is respected at the city gate, **where he takes his seat among** the elders **of the land**.

14

ADVANCE YOUR HUSBAND

> Verse 23: "Her husband is respected at the city gate, where he takes his seat among the elders of the land."

Interpretation: Her husband is popular and sits among the wise leaders of the land. She is a crown to her husband. He can boast about her. She attends to his domestic concerns. She advances her husband's interest, increases his influence. Enabling him to take his share in public matters so his name is held in high esteem, he as a great reputation.

The right woman adds to the man. Whatever he has will increase because of her. He will be elevated to high places. Whatever his purpose in life is she helps him get there. He takes his seat and everyone takes notice. She is the helpmeet, the assistant and together they make a great team. They know the help she provides, it is valued.

APPLYING: ADVANCE YOUR HUSBAND.

NEED. Men want to feel needed. A great way to advance him is to make him feel needed. He is a protector and provider. If you don't give him the opportunity to protect you or provide for you, he may feel useless. Asking for help goes a long way, even if you can do something for yourself this shows you need him. Be a damsel every now and again. Using words like respect, honor, appreciate, safe, thank you are excellent and music to their ears. Yes, works too. "Yes, please handsome."

Excerpt from my Women Series, a series of short stories: Keeping the husband first…

"The relationship between husband and wife is vital. It has to be nurtured. By making it a top priority not only do you honor God but your husband is happy. And he can function to his fullest potential making it easier for everything else to trickle down from there. So, in this case if you are living the life of a virtuous woman then you are making life at home a top priority. It's not juggling and fitting home life in, it's keeping home right and then fitting outside affairs in. Hate to break it to you but that includes work babe. I know that may be for you. I know your guy doesn't mind but if you really want him to be happy and the marriage to last forever you have to make him one number. As much as he says he's good and doesn't mind, it could take its toll over time."

COMPLIMENT. Compliment him often. Whatever he's into don't knock it. If he is into football ask him questions about it. If you're into football pretend that you don't know everything and ask him questions. If he buys something new acknowledge it and find something nice to say no matter what it is. New shirt, phone, gadget, car, hat. If he asks your opinion about choosing something be honest but nice. Material things are a man's display of himself, he needs his lady to co-sign. Find something nice to highlight no matter what it is, engage with him as he shows it off. Ask questions as he talks about it to show interest and approval. Make sure you are sincere.

FLIRT. Flirt with him. I mean this is super easy if you are totally attracted to him. Either way find something that you absolutely love about him. Flirt, flirt, flirt. Text him (not married keep it PG-13), call him when you know he's busy and leave a flirty message, right little notes and place them in places that he'll be surprised to find them (glove compartment, inside his jacket, inside a to go food container, inside a briefcase or bag or luggage). Find romantic poetry, don't recite it or communicate it all at one time, reveal it bit-by-bit. It keeps the anticipation high for the end. Create poetry of your own and make it really special. By all means flirt with your man. Keep it excitingly spicy.

"I promise to plant kisses like seeds on your body, so in time you can grow to love yourself as I love you."
TYLER KNOTT GREGSON

BLEND IN. Your husband may need you to be a chameleon. By his side at a gala. Meet his friends for a tailgate party. Attend a fancy dinner with potential clients. Host a party full of executives. You must blend in, you have to learn his world outside of the marriage. Dressing properly for the occasion but most important is the grace and elegance you exude and what comes out of your mouth. A Proverbs 31 woman knows how to master this. Her words are calculated and vital to the subject matter.

Hosting is an art and takes practice the more you do it the better you become. It's a time to be crafty and show you're really great feminine qualities. Start small like rivalry games or Super Bowl, maybe a children's party, a girlfriend's tea party or the like for practice. It will prepare you for anything your husband throws at you. Don't be afraid to hire help if needed and it works with the budget. The objective is to be flexible and blend in no matter the occasion. This further explains "Her husband is respected at the city gate, where he takes his seat among the elders of the land." Proverbs 31:23 (NIV). People respect a man whose wife honors and respects him. Make him look better than good.

Most women want time, honesty and loyalty, effort and to be made a priority. Relationships are give and take, right? So, when looking to have time, honesty and loyalty make sure you're taking care of him. To feel wanted make him feel needed. Reverence and respect him. He is necessary, his love, his presence, his energy you need it, so tell him. Might I add that a healthy man will always take care of his wife. Even when times are rough. And he will pull out the extra stops when you take great care of him. It's a win-win.

ATTENTION. Give him attention. He needs you. He needs you to interact with him. It makes me think about how it was like with Adam, the one-on-one attention he got from God. And the "Man's best friend" attention he got from all of the animals. There probably was not a huge disconnect with the animals like there is today. Since Adam was alone for a period of time, God and these creatures, he had the pleasure of naming were all he had. I can imagine the type of attention he received. Something I'm sure he got used to and needed when Eve came on the scene. Therefore, the need for attention, the sense of being "needed" is engrained in men. Same with bestiality, the tendency for males to be wild. To be brutish, indulge in beast-like appetites, instincts, impulses, etc. A Tarzan type of wild. All Adam knew was animals and his creator. He was needed for the task of human existence, of course he still has those characteristics. It's like being raised as an only child. He wants to be needed. He needs attention.

You're thinking "How does any of this stuff advance my man, my future husband? They are great suggestions and all but..." exactly, the thing is that when he feels needed and necessary, he is able to do what he needs to do. When he can recharge with love, affection and purpose (being needed and providing) he has the necessary fuel to go out and conquer the world. He can live out his purpose because his home is in order. Men fight all day to provide and justify their manhood so when he sees you it should be a reboot, a refuel. He needs the flirting, the compliments and to feel necessary. To help and assist your husband is your primary function as his wife, it is to be what he lacks.

> "Do your homework. Being a wife is an assignment."
> **LAKIA BRANDENBURG**

WHISPER SWEET EVERY-THINGS:
That looks so good on you
_____ is my favorite color on you
You are so handsome
How lucky am I
I am so blessed to have you in my life
I am honored to do life with you
I love the way you love me
You are hilarious (NOT stupid, or a fool)
You are the man
You make me better
You're the strongest man I know
They ain't got nothing on you
God is shining on you
You are so intelligent

"Happy wife, happy life? Nope, happy spouse, happy house! Men should be happy too."

JOHN MOMPLAISIR

You're a great leader
If I had to do it over again, I wouldn't change anything about us
No one does it better than you
You are the manifestation of God's love for me
I can't imagine life without you in it
I need you more than you know
You are an excellent provider
Having you in my life is necessary
It is necessary for my life to function properly, it can't without you in it
I want you around for the rest of our days
I am proud to have your last name
Life on earth is nothing without you
God whispers to me when you show me love, the display of his love through you is invaluable
To honor you is to honor God
I respect you
You're amazing
I feel so protected around you
I love the fact that I can be myself around you
You make me feel alive
Thank you for loving me
Thank you for choosing me
Thank you for being you
Thank you (ALL THE TIME)
All of me loves all of you
I LOVE YOU

To advance your husband he needs your full support. Believe in him like your life depends on it. Encourage him. Be the shoulder to lean on. Go the extra mile to make him feel like a King, the apple of your eye, the most important thing on earth to you. Give him the boost he needs. Pay attention to his patterns, language and actions, you'll know when something is off. Try your best to always stay in sync and in tune with him. Advancing your husband is a must. He is better because of you, show him why.

DAY 14
Questions

> Verse 23. "Her husband is respected at the city gate, where he takes his seat among the elders of the land."

What did you learn?

_____

_____

_____

Are you doing the necessary things for your husband to feel needed? If so, how?

_____

_____

_____

_____

Make a list of things you would say to flirt with your husband?

_____

_____

_____

_____

Single: create a list of generic flirty things:

_____

_____

_____

_____

Is your husband involved in different circles? Golf, board member, church deacon, fraternity, etc.? What ways can you vibe in his circles if necessary, how can you support him?

_____

_____

_____

_____

_____

List things you can compliment your husband on? Try adding characteristics that you love about him. Repeat the ones he responds to often.

_____

_____

_____

_____

_____

Single: create a list of generic things you can say in public about someone you are dating or your ideal husband:

_____

_____

_____

_____

How do you give him attention? Undivided attention? How can you improve?

_____

_____

_____

_____

So, you have a list of flirty things, ways to compliment him now come up with "Whisper Sweet Nothings" a little more on the sexual side. I know this may be a stretch for some but I'm sure your husband won't mind.

_____

_____

_____

_____

Books:

Now You're Speaking My Language: Honest Communication and Deeper Intimacy for a Stronger Marriage by Dr Gary Chapman

Love & War: Find Your Way to Something Beautiful in Your Marriage by John & Stasi Eldredge

100 Ways to Love Your Husband: A Life-Long Journey of Learning to Love by Lisa Jacobson

The Gift of Sex by Clifford and Joyce Penner

7 Signs You're a Married Woman Not a Wife by Lakia Bradenburg

NOTE: Lakia "LB" Brandenburg AKA "The Wife Coach" has a six-week masterclass for wives www.lakiabrandenburg.com.

Bonus Comments:

_____

_____

_____

_____

_____

_____

_____

_____

"

She makes linen garments and **sells them, and supplies** the merchants **with sashes**.

"

15

OWN YOUR OWN BUSINESS

Verse 24: "She makes linen garments and sells them, and supplies the merchants with sashes."

Interpretation: She makes products to sell and delivers or drops them off to merchants. Girdles or linen belts were more costly than leather. She creates a craft that is more profitable than selling leather, makes the fine linen to sell to merchants thus contributing to family. Back in this time it would have been a Phoenician merchant. This woman 1) made 2) delivered then 3) sold or traded the goods. She was an entrepreneur. There is no getting around the fact that she made a financial contribution to her family in addition to all the other things she offered.

I'll admit, I looked up a few things to understand this. I was surprised she created her own product and sold it. This was some kind of lady. An entrepreneur in the modern-day sense that saw it all the way through, from creating merchandise it to selling it. It's so fascinating to know that the mind-set and creativeness exist back then. It leads me to believe that it was one of the good qualities passed down. And now it's up to you to tap into your God-given creativeness.

> "If you don't build your dream, someone will hire you to help build theirs."
> TONY GASKINS, JR.

APPLYING: OWN YOUR OWN BUSINESS.

To clarify, this Proverbs 31 woman is an entrepreneur. She creates opportunities using her gifts and talents. She takes care of her husband and family. YES, I am going against what Western society has taught and continues to push, an agenda to keep families dysfunctional and apart. Too busy to come together for dinner. Replacing quality time with computers, televisions, smartphones, music and the like. Creating a wide spread disconnection with humans and an illusional connection with machines and objects. The "never satisfied" mind set, "we want more", "this isn't enough" complex. Some families are living in homes that are too large driving cars that are overpriced, buying clothes that will be only worn a handful of times each season. This fast-paced Western society lifestyle is leaving people with unfulfilled lives driving them further away from the ones that love them most. It is against what God intended. Defiant of her role as a helpmate. If you're doing more at your job than you do at home, you are out of order. Home is always first. Husband, number one.

> "Women, we're nurturers that's what expected of us, we have our children, we have our husbands if we're lucky enough but we have to find personal fulfillment, we have to follow our dreams. We have to say, I can do that and I should be allowed to do that."
> GLENN CLOSE

This is not to offend by any means. I get the fact that many women are independent and working because they are single and have no choice. I am one of them. I am trying to get you to grasp the concept of how the Heavenly Father intended it. Family Over Everything (FOE), right? Don't get too caught up in the corporate world. Focus more on your **purpose**. And by doing that you'll match up to a man that is walking in purpose as well. Know your role, why you were created and the reason God created woman. Embrace it. Create your own destiny by tapping into your God-given gifts and that is what will bring you fulfillment. Figure out how to make it lucrative while you help advance your husband, as he advances so do you.

Excerpt from *Dream Chaser* by Tony Gaskins, Jr., Author:

"You have to question the path. We all need to write our own road map that will led us to where we want to be, not where we were told we should be. Are you extremely happy doing what you're doing for a living? If not, you're on the wrong path. Are you at peace with your current lifestyle? If not, you're on the wrong path. Can you help others in the position you're currently in? If not, you're on the wrong path. If you were fired today, could you start your own company? If not, you're on the wrong path.

"...I feel that even if we work for someone else, that job should not be our dream job. If it's not our dream job, then we should build our dream job, which will eventually replace our day job."

So where is the balance? How I am all this and that to my husband and family, what about me? If corporate isn't "the move" then what am I to do? Are you artsy? Can you paint? Start painting and sell your masterpieces. You could be the next Picasso. Quilting or knitting is a cool thing to learn and something you can do for profit. Ceramics, jewelry, candles, scrubs, hand-made soap, cleaning supplies, refurbished furniture, gift baskets, flower arrangements, decorated mugs, coasters, t-shirts, cards, keychains, bookmarks, pillows, bookends, the list can go on.

My objective is to spark your built-in creativity to make things on your own, deliver and sell your goods. Pinterest is heaven when it comes to things to create and overall products you may be interested in. It is my personal go to in terms of creativity. I am inspired by the ability of others to create and to run your own business you have to be creative.

> "It's not the big things that add up in the end. It's the hundreds, thousands, or millions of little things that separate the ordinary from the extraordinary."
> **DARREN HARDY**

When thinking of what to do or whether you already have a business of your own, give something back. Create something that is meaningful and can benefit others in the long run. Yes, you can contribute to the well-being of your family and give something back as well. I love the concept of giving a portion of the proceeds to an organization or those in need. TOMS Shoes does this best with the One for One concept in which a customer's purchase benefits those in need, you buy one, they give one. It's the way it should be, life is about giving. If your sole purpose is to gain wealth, you'll never truly be wealthy. It is so much bigger than you. Find a way to give and you'll never be in need of a thing.

> "If my mind can conceive it, and my heart can believe it, then I can achieve it."
> MUHAMMAD ALI

Being an entrepreneur is more about knowing who you are and what you have to offer which should in turn correlate to a mission or the reason why you choose to do a particular thing. Find out your "why." What's your cause? What is your story? Why are you motivated to provide this product or service? Figure out what you lack or need and create it. You may find that others are in need of the exact same thing. You may have an idea, do the research to see if you're on the same page as others and that may be an opportunity to come up with something great. Perhaps it's something you learned. For example, have you experienced a tough life lesson that others can learn from? You can help guide them along their way, that could be in the form of a book, conference, blog, symposium or the like. The point isn't to create the next Fortune 500 company, per se but to live a life that helps to benefit others while creating an additional stream of income for your family. It's a way to live a meaningful and purpose filled life as you focus on family first. Don't become too involved with corporate business making someone else's dreams come true, while your family suffers by the lack of your presence.

> "No gift is too small to embrace. No gift is too small to build a business around. Anything you are gifted at can be monetized and used in a positive way."
> TONY GASKINS, JR.

ENTREPRENEUR AFFIRMATIONS: by Angel Richardson

My business allows me to live the life I want.
I work when I want, where I want, and with whom I want!
I easily attract the right clients into my business.
I visualize the success of my business and then I go make it happen!
I make an income while making an impact.

SUGGESTED WAY TO START:

> "Dreams, your imagination on steroids. Goals, steps to put in action to make your dreams become your purpose. Purpose, the overall reason you exist."
> **MS STACY LLOYD**

REALIZE YOUR PURPOSE. Figure out what your purpose is. WHAT IS YOUR WHY? What is your cause? What is your story?

I find that what you are passionate about is somehow connected to your purpose. It's starts on the inside. You already have the tools necessary to pursue your purpose. It is what God put in you. Purpose is who you are, the key is discovering who you are. Everyone is born with at least one gift or talent. Your passion is the emotion that will push you to pursue your purpose. Find your burning desire and go for it. It should be something to better humankind. It should be greater than you, more than for your selfish gain.

> "Cherish your visions and your dreams as they are the children of your soul; the blueprints of your ultimate achievements."
> **NAPOLEON HILL**

DEVELOP. Don't jump the gun, develop your purpose. You must do this before you come up with a plan to execute. It's up to you to do the research and determine what it will take to figure out a plan. Like anything you have to start somewhere. Seek those that may have some knowledge in what you are passionate about. Use all the resources you have and reach out to people who may already be successful in that area. You'd be surprised who is willing to help if you just ask. Make sure that you hone the skills necessary to start a business before you start it.

Try online courses to learn a skill or trade. Start with YouTube, a great free resource. Another option to try is Udemy, paid courses by experts in things like Health and Fitness, IT and Software, Personal Development, Marketing, Design and more. Some courses are free but most of them cost. Visit: www.udemy.com. Another sites like Skill Share, Brit + Co and SkillPop, have the same concept as Udemy. Now here's the thing with both Udemy and Skill Share you can teach courses and get paid. So, as you become an expert in your field or craft you can then structure programs to teach others what you know. Each one, teach one at its finest, you can get paid to teach. I highly suggest considering this as an option as you develop your skills. Remember, you can scale purpose.

CREATE A PLAN. When you figure out what your purpose is and develop your purpose and skill set, then you create a plan and pursue it with passion. The plan should include steps to reach goals and the deadlines to get stuff done. Your plan may need a professional business plan to get started. Everything from picking out logos, to social media handles, website design, business license, incorporation, to trademarks and copyrights, they should all be included in your plan. The more you do the more you can continue to move forward in the direction of your plan and ultimately your purpose.

Don't mistake dreams for goals, they are different. *Goals are defined as an object of a person's ambition of effort an aim or desired result.* They are steps that you take to achieve your dreams. Goals are measurable steps with deadlines, oftentimes requiring money, as well as measure your gradual progress to reach your dreams.

> "A dream written down with a date becomes a goal. A goal broken down unto steps becomes a plan. A plan backed by action becomes reality."
> GREG REID

GOALS:
S-Specific, be specific about your goals
M-Measurable, your goals should be measured
A-Attainable, goals must be reachable
R-Relevant, needs to connect with your overall dream
T-Timed, goals have deadline so make sure you create them

ASPIRATION MOUNTAIN

Create dreams that will last a lifetime, you can add goals to help you reach them. It's all about being happy and having something to live and reach for. Don't live your life without dreams and aspirations. Don't sit on your dreams, give them the attention they deserve.

Dreams are a series of thoughts and ideas connected to your imagination and soul. Here's the thing, you may have more than one dream. If you have more than one talent chances are, you'll have more than one dream. Your big dream should take a lifetime of goals to reach leading to and fulfilling your ultimate purpose.

Your purpose is the reason you were born. It's passion in action baby! One dream can have lots of goals in order to accomplish over time. It is important to figure out what your big dream is, after you do that you can create a plan to execute. The plan includes goals, start with small and continue to progress to get you closer to your specific dream.

Try using an aspiration mountain to help you get started on your goals. Use the blank illustration and completed versions for inspiration.

ASPIRATION MOUNTAIN

SPEAK AROUND THE GLOBE

RESOURCES TO GET BOOKED

SPEAKING IN SMALL GROUPS

FEAR, PROCRASTINATION, NEGATIVITY, DOUBT, PUBLIC VALIDATION

Talent/Gift —>Goals —>Dreams = Purpose

> "A real decision is measured by the fact that you've taken a new action. If there's no action, you haven't truly decided."
> **TONY ROBBINS**

USE RESOURCES. There are free resources that you can use to help get you started. All social media accounts can help to get the word out for any cause or mission. Solicit the help of interns. See if you can barter services. There are small business grants and loans out there. If you need help ask. Try crowd-funding to raise money for a business or pursue a dream. GoFundMe, Kickstarter and Indiegogo. Use your resources. And don't allow anything in life to derail you from your dreams.

> "Being who you are is power. It's walking in your purpose. It's being who you were designed to be. You were created for a mission, be you."
> MS STACY LLOYD

EXECUTE. Faith without works is dead. You must execute what you set out to do. Anything less is waste of skin. In essence, you're not living or working toward your purpose. Continue to learn and grow, make plans, reach goals and do it over and over again. You can write books and eBooks, have live webinars, create a podcast, blog or vlog. Teach classes, organize retreats or conferences, the possibilities to scale are broad. Remember that by walking in your purpose you give others the freedom to be able to do the same. Don't delay, start now.

> "Never limit yourself because of others limited imagination; never limit others because of your own limited imagination."
> DR. MAE JEMISON

HAVING YOUR OWN BUSINESS:

HOME BUSINESSES: These business models are already created to help women contribute to their families while allowing flexibility to nurture what's most important.

Chloe + Isabel Jewelry
Traci Lynn Fashion Jewelry
stella & dot
AVON
Mary Kay
Paparazzi Accessories

SELL YOUR STUFF:

You can create things and sell them for purchase. This is an awesome way to bring in money to help contribute to the family. Sell at your local outdoor farmer's market, festivals, do a pop-up shop or try setting up in heavy pedestrian traffic areas and sell yourself. Use Square, Clover Go, Cash App, Apple Pay, PayPal or other apps to accept purchases.

SUGGESTED VIRTUAL PLACES TO SELL ITEMS:

Etsy

Fiverr

Homemade at Amazon

Handmadeology

eBay

Zazzle

Zibbet

Handmade Artists

Made it Myself (MiM)

Shopify

BigCommerce

Uncommongoods

The Grommet (They launch undiscovered products
and help them succeed)

Chairish (consignment-based app good for selling artwork and décor)

PLACES TO TAKE CLASSES:

Michael's Craft Stores

Home Depot

Lowe's

Brit + Co (Online Classes)

Udemy (Online Classes)

Skill Share (Online Classes)

SkillPop (Online Classes)

SUGGESTED WEBSITES TO USE:

Build Your Website:

Squarespace www.squarspace.com (Website Building Site)

Word Press www.wordpress.com (Website + Blog Building Site)

WIX www.wix.com (Website Building Site)

Marketing Tools:
MailChimp www.mailchimp.com
(For Marketing + Mass Email Subscriptions)
HootSuite www.hootsuite.com
(Scheduling Multiple Social Media Post Simultaneously)
Later www.later.com (Scheduling Instagram Post)
Quirky www.quirky.com
(Submit your invention to community, get genius feedback)
Grammarly www.grammarly.com (FREE writing website and app to
eliminate grammar mistakes)
Dribbble (Self-promotion platform for digital designers)

Creative Inspiration:
Pinterest www.pinterest.com
Mollie Makes www.molliemakes.com
Real Simple www.realsimple.com
Southern Living www.southernliving.com

SUPPORTIVE BUSINESS GROUPS:
National Association of Women Business Owners www.nawbo.org
National Association for Business Resources www.nationalbiz.org
National Federation of Independent Business www.nfib.com
Small Business Administration www.sba.gov

SUGGESTED HOME/DIY VIDEOS TO WATCH:

You can watch these videos to help come up with some really cool ideas for stuff to make and possibly sell. You can make gifts or create things to decorate around the house. There are some really good start-up business friendly videos. If you have a Facebook page this is how I access videos from the list below. You just plug in the name in the search section and the pages will pop up. Look for their videos and enjoy.

Pop Sugar: Home
Nifty
Country Living Magazine
5-Minute Crafts

Refinery29 Living
Michael's Stores

SOCIAL MEDIA IMPACT:

I highly recommend the use of social media for business. For starters it's
FREE. Social media is a great way to reach your target audience through
marketing. Each platform offers different aspects of social media and
different audiences you can tap into. The platform you choose to use or
focus on depends on your target customer. Utilizing all platforms will
cover you and yield the most benefits. I use all of the below but as trends
change, and will continue to change, it is best to pay attention to see what
adjustments you may need to make.

Facebook: connect with past and current friends, family, classmates, co-
workers and more. It is a great way to let your tribe know what business
adventure you are working on. Share photos and videos, send messages
and get updates, sell items in the marketplace. Create a business page that
is connected to your personal page and encourage folks to follow and like
the page, it's a great way to engage with users that use this platform. And
if you're pushing content try Facebook Watch or Facebook Live.

Twitter: online news and social networking, where users "tweet" their
thoughts in 280 characters or less. This platform has proven to be great
for Health and Wellness, Business, Wealth, Tech and Sports industries,
Celebrities and Politics.

Instagram: a photo and video-sharing social networking service owned by
Facebook, Inc. This is a good way to visually capture your audience and
direct them to your site.

LinkedIn: professional business and employment service network. It's
used by companies and individuals as a way to showcase their talent
or seek talent. It can include employers posting jobs and job seekers
posting resumes, information sharing, connection building, relationship
nurturing. This site and app can be used to spread the word about your
business.

YouTube: video sharing website. Another visual platform but second to Google as a top search engine, top three websites globally. In fact, it's owned by Google. This service can be used to provide how-to and marketing videos, shows and more. Create your own YouTube channel and push to have people subscribe.

Pinterest: helps you discover what you love. This site and app allow you to "pin" photos to save for inspiration, like having a digital vision board. You can find just about anything and it is an awesome way to create and boards of your own photos for marketing your business and products that link directly to your website. Primarily used by women, this is a great too if this is your audience.

PEOPLE AND COMPANIES TO FOLLOW
ON INSTAGRAM + TWITTER:

@Entrepreneur
@BusinessInsider
@WallStreetJournal
@Forbes
@FortuneMagazine
@AmericanExpress (They have a program for Small Businesses)
@HuffingtonPost
@TechCrunch
@NYTimes
@TheEconomist
@bumblebizz
@paulcbrunson
@SoFi
@OnDeckCapital
@ienrichher

> "You don't have to be rich to give back and you don't have to retire to spend every day doing what you love. You can find profit, passion, and meaning all at once—right now."
>
> **BLAKE MYCOSKIE**

10 DAILY HABITS OF MOST SUCCESSFUL ENTREPRENEURS:

CREATE A ROUTINE
DO THE HARDEST TASK FIRST
EXERCISE AND MEDITATE
PREP FOR THE FOLLOWING DAY
KEEP LEARNING
STRIVE FOR SOLUTIONS
KEEP TRACK OF YOUR PROGRESS. STAY TASK ORIENTED
INCLUDE REVENUE GENERATING ACTIVITIES
RECHARGE. SPEND TIME WITH LOVED ONES
DIVIDE EACH DAY FOR DIFFERENT BUSINESS ACTIVITIES

"Conditions are never perfect. "Someday" is a disease that will take your dreams to the grave with you."

TIMOTHY FERRISS

DAY 15

Questions

> Verse 24. "She makes linen garments and sells them, and supplies the merchants with sashes."

What did you learn from this chapter?

_____

_____

_____

What is your opinion about full-time working wives and mothers?

_____

_____

_____

What qualifies the Proverbs 31 woman to be an entrepreneur by today's definition?

_____

_____

_____

_____

In your opionon what is the difference between passion and purpose?

_____

_____

_____

Make a list of things that you'd be passionate enough to make from home?

_____

_____

_____

Do you know your purpose?

_____

_____

_____

What can you do to serve others and live out your purpose?

_____

_____

_____

_____

Is there something that you can do full-time to bring money in the household?

_____

_____

_____

Create a list of resources you'd use to start your own business from the book:

_____

_____

_____

Make a plan to achieve a few goals that will get you to your dreams and eventually purpose:

_____

_____

_____

What habits can you do each day that will assist in your success.

_____

_____

_____

Make a list of your own affirmations pertaining to business, say them out loud daily:

_____

_____

_____

Books:
The Purpose Driven Life by Rick Warren
Dream Chaser by Tony Gaskins
The Entrepreneur Roller Coaster by Darren Hardy
The Entrepreneur's Startup Gameplan by Sharon Beason
Think and Grow Rich by Napoleon Hill
The Law of Success by Napoleon Hill
The 21 Irrefutable Laws of Leadership by John C. Maxwell
The 4-Hour Workweek by Timothy Ferriss
Congratulations! It's a Brand by Dr. Melva Robertson
You are a Badass by Jen Sincero
Influence by Robert Cialdini
Pre-suasion by Robert Cialdini
Essentialism by Greg McKeown

Bonus Comments:

_____

_____

_____

_____

_____

She is clothed with strength and dignity; she **can laugh** at the **days to come**.

16

BE CONFIDENT

> Verse 25: "She is clothed with strength and dignity; she can laugh at the days to come."

Interpretation: Strength and honor cloth her. She wears strength and dignity and because of that she smiles at her future. And she rejoices at the time to come. She is intertwined with a mortal force and dignity that arm her against care or worry. The power of a righteous purpose and strong will, she revels in her demeanor she laughs and rejoices, doesn't worry of what may happen knowing whom she serves.

She is far from insecure; she is completely confident about what her role and position is as a woman and she walks in it. She doesn't waiver from her duties and is happy about life. The future, she's got it covered to the point worry and stress are far from her mind. She laughs because she knows that she's done her part and God meets her where she lacks.

> "The woman who does not require validation from anyone is the most feared individual on the planet."
> **MOHADESA NAJUMI**

I am not a one in a million kind of girl. I am a once in a lifetime kind of woman. I am unique. I am wonderfully made. There is no one like me, past, present or in the future. Every hair on my head is numbered. That makes me special and like no other. God took great detail in creating me all before the world was formed. You are no exception. You are the human manifestation of his greatness. You're legendary, you're extraordinary so own it.

That is the type of confidence you should have each day. Your uniqueness is what makes you, you. It is like a badge of honor. Trust me you are fantastic. When you know it, it's confidence in its purest form. *Confidence, is self-assuring of one's own abilities. It is state of feeling certain about the truth of something.* It's like you know, that you know, that you know, that you are awesome.

> "I was once afraid of people saying, "who does she think she is?" Now I have the courage to stand and say, "This is who I am."
>
> OPRAH

APPLYING: BE CONFIDENT.

Let me be clear, being confident has nothing to do with being popular. It has absolutely nothing to do with your social media accounts. How many followers you have, likes you get, retweets, hashtags, trending topic feeds you land on, magazine covers you grace, websites or columns you might be featured in. People do not have the power to dictate your confidence and popularity is not what makes you confident. Please don't let the media and the public at large fool you, they don't dictate how you feel about yourself. *Confident, to be self-assured. Feeling or showing certainty, positive, self-reliant, self-possessed.* There you have it, SELF, it is up to you to embody confidence, it is an inside job. Just like your happiness it's up to you to believe in yourself in order to develop confidence.

> "And let not your adornment be merely external-braiding the hair, and wearing gold jewelry, or putting on dresses; but let it be the hidden person of the heart, with the imperishable quality of a gentle and quiet spirit, which is precious in the sight of God."
>
> PETER 3:3-4 (NIV)

Confidence should not be wrapped up in the clothes you put on, the make-up you wear, shoes you slide into or the purse you carry. It should not be the house you live in, the car you drive or the tangible in general. It's not about being pretty and flaunting around. The external and outward appearance are far from what should be represented. What is on the inside should come out, it's really the energy you give. Have you ever watched a confident woman? She is naturally accepting of herself.

> "We get so worried about being "pretty"...lets be pretty kind, pretty funny, pretty smart, pretty strong."
> JENESSA WAIT

Being confident is being sure of yourself. It is the ability to know who you are and be both satisfied and comfortable with it. It's owning you, the embracement of the essence of you, your internal self as well as your external. It is to walk in the peace of knowing who you are and why you came. Confidence is to sprinkle glitter on everyone you meet and never letting them forget that you came and you conquered. Confidence is saying what needs to be said with love and dropping the mic. Confidence is YOU.

> "Confidence, charisma, and character outshine any beauty."
> COCO HO

EXUDE CONFIDENCE:

THINK. To be confident starts in the mind. You really have to know, that you know, that you know that you are what you believe you are. That starts with your thoughts. I remember hearing once that if you want to become something you have to believe that you are already that thing. *Belief, an acceptance that a statement is true or that something exists.* I called myself an author before I actually became one. I see myself on every bestsellers list, ultimately to help the masses. You must believe you are, it starts in the mind. It's a basic law of attraction. Do what you can to change your thinking to positive and uplifting things and think with confidence.

> "Your chances of success in any undertaking can always be measured by your belief in yourself."
> ROBERT COLLIER

SPEAK. This goes right along with belief. You must speak life, speak those things that are not as though they are. Birth great things in your life with the words you say. What you give life to will grow so you have to be mindful of what you say. The awesome thing is that you have the power to control what you say. And by that you control what you give life to. Words are all so mighty and can change the vibrations of fluid movement. They can be destructive and disruptive. Be careful what you say. You want the use of words to work on your behalf. Walk in the authority that God has given you, you have the power to speak with confidence.

ACT. A closed mouth doesn't get fed. You not only have to believe and speak but you have to act. Confidence will take you places your mind might not have imagined you'd go. Stepping out on faith is courageous and admirable. And being confident is not for the timid or weak at heart. It is the step necessary to get things going. A woman that is confident is willing to take steps to make things happen. She is a go-getter, she doesn't wait for a push to go she just goes. She is led by the spirit and moves with confidence, in sync and in-line. She doesn't battle with what she believes, she speaks with the upmost respect and grace, she walks with steps of intention and action.

All of the above is inside of you. You just have to learn to tap into it, if you already haven't. It is blind faith in my opinion. You'll never get anywhere if you don't take a step. Sometimes you'll have to take a jump because a step won't do what is required of you to get to the next level God is taking you. Steps are testing the water were as jumps are diving right in and taking the coldness like a champ. If you don't act on a thing it is less than confident. I know you've got it in you to conquer so act on it.

> "Courage is a love affair with the unknown."
> OSHO

COURAGE. To have courage is the ability to do something that scares the living daylights out of you. It frightens you but you choose to overcome your fears and do it anyway. It's the difference between taking steps and jumping. Steps vs jumping, steps are to take action is to do something. To take the steps to move forward or to complete a task.

To have courage is jumping in total faith. It is saying "I don't know what will happen but I have the courage to try," then you just jump. Courage is a great virtue, it's ruthless, hardcore in a sense, it is being fearless. It is thinking about the odds, not caring and jumping anyway. Courage is living life without regret. A confident woman is one with courage and never waivers on her abilities or the days to come.

YOU. Be you. There is nothing more confident than being yourself. You are you. No one can take that away. No two people are just alike, not even identical twins. It is so awesome knowing that there is just one Stacy. There is only one of me special and unique. That before the world was formed God had me in mind. That gives me so much life. Think about the magnitude of that. You are one of a kind, no human is or will ever be YOU. There is so much power in knowing you are created on purpose for a purpose. You must not let it go to waste. Don't bury your gifts. Be you.

> "If I don't poke my head out of my shell and show people who I am, all anyone will ever think I am is my shell."
> **SHONDA RHIMES**

Knowing yourself is vital in moving forward in life. Not getting older. By merely being alive you're getting older. To really live a fulfilled life, you must know who you are. When you know who you are you can live a life of purpose. Each day you are walking in your destiny, a life fulfilled. If you don't know who you are you are not living you are merely existing. You are not learning and developing the gifts and talents God gave you. In reality, you have buried them. Your gifts are inside, see them through by being what God put in you. Everything you need you already possess. That's what confidence is, self-possession. You own what you possess. You can't do or be anyone other than you.

I have to say this, please don't emulate others. A peer, friends, mentor or celebs. Celebs have a lot of influence I get it. Popularity gives the illusion that celebs are people to envy and model yourself after. It's great to admire someone but be mindful of what you admire. If admiration is the force that draws you to someone ask yourself about their character. Instead of looking at their outward appearance look inside. That is what should be acknowledged and highlighted. Remember to praise The Creator and not what is created. And always show empathy, it's the ability to see someone where they are without judgement. It's best to lend your heart to theirs. Most importantly, never forget to be you. You are fantastic. You are good.

> "Don't ask what the world needs. Ask what makes you come alive and go do it. Because what the world needs is people who have come alive."
> **HOWARD WASHINGTON THURMAY**

PERSONAL AFFIRMATIONS:

I AM ONE OF A KIND
I CAN DO ANYTHING I PUT MY MIND TO
WHAT I HAVE TO OFFER NO ONE ELSE CAN
THERE IS NO ONE LIKE ME
I AM SPECIAL
I CELEBRATE MY OWN INDIVIDUALITY
I AM LOVE
GOD AND I, WE GOT THIS
GOD CREATED ME IN HIS IMAGE
GOD CREATED ME BEFORE THE HEAVENS AND EARTH
I WAS CREATED FOR A PURPOSE
I AM ENOUGH
I AM POWERFUL
I AM CONFIDENT

> "With confidence you have won before you have started."
> **MARCUS GARVEY**

DAY 16
Questions

> Verse 25. "She is clothed with strength and dignity; she can laugh at the days to come."

What did you learn from this chapter?

_____

_____

_____

What would you tell your 10-year-old self about confidence?

_____

_____

_____

How would you rate your confidence on a scale from 1 to 10, 10 being the highest? And why?

_____

_____

_____

_____

How do you think you can improve?

_____

_____

_____

_____

Write a list of personal affirmations to build your confidence. Use the example from this chapter as a guide:

_____

_____

_____

_____

Based on the list of personal affirmations you create from above, write them down and repeat them two times a day. Perhaps you can put them in your phone and have reminders sent. Take a dry erase marker and put a few on the bathroom mirror or try Post-It notes where you can see them frequently. The point is to get in the habit of affirming yourself thus building your confidence.

_____

_____

_____

_____

Books:
The Women's Book of Confidence by Sue Patton Thoele
Self-Confidence by Paul McGee
The Little Book of Confidence by Susan Jeffers
The Confident Woman Devotional: 365 Daily Inspirations by Joyce Meyer
You Are a Badass by Jen Sincero

Bonus Comments:

_____

_____

_____

_____

_____

_____

_____

_____

"

She speaks with wisdom, and faithful instruction is on her tongue.

"

17

SPEAK WISELY

> Verse 26: "She speaks with wisdom, and faithful instruction is on her tongue."

Interpretation: She opens her mouth and speaks wisdom. Her tongue is the law of kindness. Like she defines kindness, look in the dictionary and bam a P31 woman is there.

She chooses her words wisely. No fussing, no slander or idle talk but of prudence (cautiousness) and sound sense. She is discrete, she loves and is kind with grace and empathy. This woman doesn't talk just to be talking. She is thoughtful and calculated in the way she communicates her thoughts and feelings. She is far removed from emotions and her ego therefore she does not speak with intent to harm. Expression of her feelings is wise and in tune because she understands her emotions so she can state how she feels without offense. She speaks from a place of empathy and compassion. This allows for better resolutions to problems as a result. She is the ultimate good communicator.

APPLYING: SPEAK WISELY.

A wise woman will know when and what to say at the appropriate time. She is able to use discernment to know to whom she is speaking, when to say what needs to be said and exactly what to communicate.

You are a nurturer by design and you assist in development. In order to properly "teach" you must come from a place of love and kindness. Like that of a mother to her newborn, she is gentle and careful in every way. This is the best way to communicate. Be soft, think about how you'd like to be spoken to. Be gentle.

> "Gracious words are like a honeycomb, sweetness to the soul and health to the bones."
> PROVERBS 16:24 (NIV)

LEARN HOW TO SPEAK WITH GRACE:

TONE. When speaking, use a soothing tone. It's not what you say but how you say it. You'll find that people are more receiving of what you say when your tone is at a low level and the energy is rooted in love and kindness. Honor your husband when communicating. If you think of a husband as a representation of God on earth, your tone would be gentle, respectful and kind. Start conversations off with uplifting words of admiration, praise and honor and then whatever needs to be addressed in the most kind and gentle way. This should help with conflicts, try keep them to a minimum as well.

COMMUNICATION. Don't say "We need to talk." Oh dear God, I said this once to a guy I was dating and he flipped. It was as if the world was about to end. And he told me, never to say it again and I haven't to him or in any other relationship since. Try "Let's chat" or "Let's discuss" maybe "Can I ask you something?" But never "We need to talk." It can put a man or the person for that matter on the defense. Like what did I do wrong?

Be mindful of generalizing words "always" or "never", address a specific issue, remember to be kind and loving. Watch how you say things, refrain from insults and words that are negative or have an undertone that you're putting him down. The point is to talk and always keep the lines of communication open. Being 100% honest and free of judgement.

> "The wise store up knowledge, but the mouth of a fool invites ruin."
> PROVERBS 10:14 (NIV)

Find the proper time to discuss things, when either person is emotional or egos are present it is generally not the best time. Remove emotions and egos and then come together to discuss with level heads. Find a neutral zone in the house that is off limits to bad energy. Like the bedroom or the bed for that matter. Create a space of tranquility that will not be subject to anything less than a state of peace. Work hard at maintaining that space. Always talk, always stay connected.

GRATITUDE. Gratitude is the best attitude, always. When you are in the full-time business of giving thanks, you attract good energy and great things come back to you. Having a heart of gratitude applies to everything in life. Your relationship with others especially your husband is no different. Look at the people around you, what they add to your life is a blessing. I believe that those closest to you are a reflection of you. They are people that God sent for one reason or another. Those relationships are meant to be managed with care. I also believe that they are a reflection of God's love for you. I'm talking real genuine and healthy relationships. Your husband, family and friends are a gift and that's enough to be grateful for.

Gratitude is a great foundation to communicating and speaking wisely. The more you can find to appreciate, the less anything else matters. Being grateful is imperative, it sets the tone for goodness.

> "I define joy as a sustained sense of well-being and internal peace- a connection to what matters."
> **OPRAH WINFREY**

REQUEST. Ask and ye shall receive, right? I think it's about how you ask. No one wants to do something for someone that is overly demanding. Someone that wants you to do something for them when they want you to do it. Sounds like a mother doesn't it. Ha! I'll leave mothers out of this; we're talking husband and wife here. No husband wants a nagging wife. A wife that is demanding and can't properly speak and make a request. No need to do a survey on this topic. Watch how you request. Do not nag.

LISTEN. Men tell you where they are at and what they feel, please listen. Listen and take them seriously. Men don't talk or communicate the way women do. In fact, men talk less during the day then women. I think it's because of the way that we communicate. We have 50 million things going on in our heads that in order to really express ourselves we have to use tons of words. Guys are simple, straight to the point no chaser. So, with that in mind women must really pay attention. If it's coming out of his mouth, he means it. If he's writing it, he means it. Don't be in denial. Believe him. Listen. And if he is communicating something he needs or wants try your best to meet the request and be there for him. When you don't listen, you disconnect from him. He wants to be heard just like you.

WAYS YOU CAN SPEAK:

- Speak to uplift. Stay away from insults and belittling him, it will not get you anywhere. In fact, things may end up worse based on your delivery.

- Gently. Like the tone you use when talking to a baby. Use a gentle tone.

- Listen. You have to listen, really listen in order to determine your response and figure out what the need is. Pay attention. Men talk, you just have to listen and take them seriously. Men talk, you just have to listen and take them seriously. Use this acronym to remember the purpose of listening:

Listen
Intently
Silently
To
Explore
Need

NOTE: LISTEN and SILENT have the same letters

- Respond don't react. Responses are thought out where as a reaction is more based on emotions. Reactions are your first feeling in reference to a particular situation. The slight difference is emotion. Don't get so caught up in your emotions and your feelings that you speak in an offensive manner. Take the time to think then respond. Use "Can you excuse me for a moment?" It gives you a chance to gather yourself. I like to say a silent prayer in my head and ask God for help so that I can respond properly and with kindness at all cost.

"Sin is not ended by multiplying words, but the prudent hold their tongues. The tongue of the righteous is choice silver, but the heart of the wicked is of little value."

PROVERBS 10:19-20 (NIV)

DAY 17

Questions

> Verse 26. "She speaks with wisdom, and faithful instruction is on her tongue."

Jot down what you took from this chapter?

_____

_____

_____

Do you speak with wisdom and gentleness?

_____

_____

_____

_____

What can you do to improve?

_____

_____

_____

How do you express your gratitude to others? Your husband?

_____

_____

_____

Do you know the best form of communication your husband uses? It may closely tie into his love language. Again, I highly recommend that you read *The 5 Love Languages* by Gary Chapman.

_____

_____

_____

Create a list of ways you can better listen to your husband:

_____

_____

_____

Single: Create a list of ways you can listen to those you engage with the most:

_____

_____

_____

Books:
How to Say It Rosalie Maggio
How to Talk so Your Husband Will Listen: And Listen So Your Husband Will Talk by Rick Johnson
Love & Respect by Dr. Emerson Eggerichs
Picture Perfect by LaKia Brandenburg

Bonus Comments:

_____

_____

_____

_____

_____

_____

_____

"

She watches over the affairs of her household and does not eat the bread of idleness.

"

18

STAY BUSY + ALERT

> Verse 27: "She watches over the affairs of her household and does not eat the bread of idleness."

Interpretation: She watches the home and doesn't partake in idleness. She is in constant awareness for her family and keeping an eye on their actions and habits. There isn't a lazy bone in her body. She wisely manages the house, busy but with the right things so she is resourceful with her time. They say "If you don't work you don't eat" so she labors for her husband and family. And she diligently tries to do what is right and will not do things that ultimately won't serve the household.

APPLYING: STAY BUSY + ALERT.

Your household is your number one priority. Be in sync with your femininity and know your role as first a wife and then a mother, putting all other things aside to care for the family. Clearly this is challenging in American society however, you may need to make life adjustments in order to accomplish this. Try to cutdown extracurricular activities, get a part time job instead of a full-time gig to ensure the home is number one. Your husband above all, he is a direct reflection of your love for God on earth. The attention must be given to him (including sexually on a regular basis) and after your husband then the children.

There is not time nor do you designate time to sit idle, make sure to constantly check on the affairs of the house and that things in the house are operating properly. I believe that even if you aren't present (date night, a quick errand without kids, travel or a "self-care" day) you can secure someone responsible to handle things temporarily in your brief absence. But always knows what's happening in your home, it should be a top priority.

WAYS TO STAY BUSY:

ACTIVE. Stay active. I've already given tips on how to stay physically active. This type of active is all inclusive to the impact you have in your community or organizations that help foster unity. Keep fighting the good fight to help the youth become good men and women. Help not only giving to the needy, that's one component but positively impacting humanity. It's about building a network of like-minded people for the common goal of upbuilding the Kingdom of God. Stay active in your work for the Kingdom.

This is no lazy woman. Yes, she is busy but she knows how to balance it all. She is aware of living a complete and fulfilled life. She has no time to waste on things that do not serve her. She refuses to be idle. To be *idle, is not active in use, not working, unemployed, lazy.* This is far from the woman that is praised by her husband, family and those that gather at the gates of the city. She works and she works hard. So, don't slave, utilize you time wisely. Refrain from wasting your time with gossip, small talk, water cooler stories, soap operas, guilty pleasures or anything that really doesn't serve you or your family. Learn how to really make good use of your 24-hours.

> "The most effective way to do it, is to do it."
> **AMELIA EARHART**

ALERT. *Consciousness, it is the ability to stay connected to the mind of God.* The connection between your mind and God's mind. Her consciousness is a blessing and it is unlimited. To be aligned with the Creator of all is to be alert and aware of the things around you. It is knowing what is going on in your community, city, state, country and the world. To know what is happening to better prepare your family. To know what you need to execute. Be hip and know the latest trends and happenings but make sure you know what's going on behind closed doors. Things like government policies, zoning, education, taxes, etc. Don't isolate yourself, seek knowledge and be alert.

CALCULATED. She has intention and goes after it. She is focused on family and to be anything other than busy is not an option. She has no idea what idle time is, she's active. Be calculated and strategize what is best for your husband and family. Be ahead of the game know what's going on and forecast an action plan for the future. And because you know what going on, this is a breeze. Have good time management so that you are able to juggle your life with ease.

> "The woman who follows the crowd will usually go no further than the crowd. The woman who walks alone is likely to find herself in places no one has been before."
> **ALBERT EINSTEIN**

EVOLVE. Growth is critical to a P31 woman. She is always evolving. She understands the need to improve, learn and develop. She is constantly searching for ways to improve. Do not allow excuses to hinder or stifle your growth. Seek assistance to help in your evolution of self. The notion of self-mastery is not foreign to you, you just embrace it with pride and continue to evolve to new heights.

FOCUS. In order to get things done you have to be focused. This woman was busy but can focus in on what needs to be done at any given time. She can hone in on the task at hand and execute. You have the ability to block out the noise in order to complete the job. Don't allow distractions or circumstances to derail you. See the road ahead and fixate yourself on the prize. Be head strong and determined.

> "Effort is the route available to the underdog. I may not be able to outspend you. But I can outwork you."
> **MALCOLM GLADWELL**

STAY ALERT:

Proper sleep:
You need energy. Make sure you're getting enough sleep. Shut things down and get on a routine to get the proper 7-9 hours. Don't sleep near electronics and do something relaxing to wind down.

Exercise:
If you need a boost exercising will help fuel energy. If you exercise daily it will help you sleep when your body has to recharge.

Nutrition:
Proper nutrition will give you energy. How do vegans' function at full capacity if they only eat fruits and vegetables? Yes, exactly. Eating healthy will aid in giving you the energy to stay active throughout the day.

Vitamins:
Vitamins will also help give you nutrients that your body needs to rejuvenate itself in order to stay alert.

Meditate:
It helps to clear out the mind. If your mind is clear you can then be more productive with the things you need to focus on. Try a guided meditation or sit in stillness.

DAY 18
Questions

> Verse 27. "She watches over the affairs of her household and does not eat the bread of idleness."

What did you learn from this chapter?

_____

_____

_____

Are there areas in your home that can use more attention?

_____

_____

_____

_____

Make a list of those areas that require more of your attention:

_____

_____

_____

_____

Create a schedule to make time for those areas:

_____

_____

_____

_____

_____

What could you do to minimize your idle time? Is there a way to multi-task? Try watching a TV show and folding clothes.

_____

_____

_____

_____

What can you do to prioritize things at home?

_____

_____

_____

_____

Books:

The Tipping Point: How Little Things Can Make a Big Difference by Malcolm Gladwell

Intentional Living: Choosing a Life that Matters by John C. Maxwell

Bonus Comments:

_____

_____

_____

_____

_____

_____

_____

_____

Her children **arise** and call **her blessed**; her husband also, **and he praises** her.

19

ENJOY YOUR FRUITFULNESS

| Verse 28: "Her children arise and call her blessed; her husband also, and he praises her."

Interpretation: Her kids and hubby call her blessed. She is fantastic and owns her role as a wife and mother. She is fruitful and as a result she is acknowledged. It's like a gold star, medal or badge of honor for her faithfulness to her family.

To bear fruit is to see the "fruits of your labor." To experience the manifestation of what you planted. If the fruit is not planted in good soil it will not grow. So, for this P31 woman to be praised it is the manifestation of the good seeds she planted to make sure that her husband and family were taken care of. Otherwise there would be no fruit, no evidence of the good she planted and certainly no praise.

APPLYING: ENJOY YOUR FRUITFULNESS.

Bask in the fruits of your labor. That may mean taking "me" time. I encourage it to be "me" time. A Proverbs 31 woman will always know when it is time to recharge. She knows that in order to give in the capacity that is needed she must not draw from an empty cup she must refuel. You can't function with a low and empty cup because will not benefit anyone. In fact, it is detrimental to everyone if you are not full. You must keep in mind the essence of having a balanced life. It allows you to operate at full capacity in order to give to others.

ENJOY THE FRUITS OF YOUR LABOR:

REST. Honey you have got to know when to chill out. Learn the art of listening to your body. It will tell you when you need to rest, if you don't take heed then your body will shut itself down and force you to rest. It usually comes in the form of some sickness, minor or major, temporary or fatal. Therefore, it is imperative that you listen to your body and rest. You should be getting proper rest which is a recommended 7-9 hours per night. Outside of that you need to pay close attention to your body. Proper sleep is needed to function but is also necessary even when it comes to weight loss, as mentioned in chapter 8. Your body needs time to heal itself. That happens when you sleep. Enjoy the fruits of your labor and rest.

Know when it's time to solicit the help of others to get rest. Don't run yourself crazy because you have to do everything yourself. Delegate or hire someone to help so that you can get the proper rest. If you are on empty you don't serve anyone. It is useless for everyone if you have nothing to give.

SELF-CARE. Now this is the fun part. This entails taking care of yourself. This is regularly scheduled appointments to keep you feeling rejuvenated and feminine. Hair or nail appointments, massages, facials, and any pampering of all sorts. It is also taking out the time

> "Rest and self-care are so important. When you take time to replenish your spirit it allows you to serve others from the overflow. You cannot serve from an empty vessel."
>
> ELEANOR BROWN

to recharge. Sleeping is one thing but you may have to take a few days and center yourself. Take a solo trip, become one with nature, go to a retreat or conference, you can read a book, devote more time to meditate, practice yoga. Whatever it takes to fill yourself back up. You may not always get what you need to refuel you from any one person. I know it'd be nice if your husband could but that may not be the case. That is why it's important to disconnect and take care of self, that's why it's called SELF-care.

DISCONNECT. Even a woman who is always "on" needs a break. You can't do it all of the time. Having the ability to disconnect is a gem. And when I say disconnect, I mean unplug. Put the care of your family in trusted hands, turn the phone on mute, don't answer emails, no social media, no television shows to catch up on, no movies, no Netflix, Prime, Hulu or the others. Completely shut out the outside world, that is really disconnecting. The world will go on if you don't have your hand in everything. If you've put the care of loved ones in trusted hands then relax. Pre-plan for it, work ahead to ensure that you won't be bothered unless it's an emergency. Make this a habit and won't be the end of the world when you need to disconnect. You set the boundaries and structure. The more you stick with it everyone else will too.

JOY. Do things that give you joy. That energy and feeling of joy ignites good things. If you add love to it then it sends you over the moon. These are high frequencies. You are energy, you send out your vibrations without even speaking a word. And the more you are doing things that bring you joy the more you exude joy. That joy and happiness coupled with love come out and put people in a trance of the same. It's truly contagious. That is what you want to spread, joy, happiness and love. It comes back to you.

NOW. There is no time like the present. Enjoy life now. Take in each moment. Tomorrow is not promised and there is no time like today. Savor this time, embrace where you are in life and be thankful for it. You've done the work and now is the time to bask in the accomplishment of doing an excellent job. Having gratitude for where you are now is important in getting more of the same if not better. Learn to enjoy the now.

FRUITS OF LABOR:

- Reward yourself:
  Whatever makes you feel good, do that. It's like working really hard and getting paid then buying that shirt you've been eyeing for a while. It's taking a long walk in nature 60-miles away from your surroundings to get some fresh air and recharge.

- Travel:
  Go somewhere you've never been before. The saying is, "Work hard. Play hard." You should go on a trip somewhere you've never been at least once a year. Either a solo trip or a trip with girlfriends to stay in your feminine grace. Take a long weekend or a week.

> "Travel brings power and love back to your life."
> RUMI

I love to travel. In a perfect world I'd travel the globe and write. And now it's in the atmosphere so we'll see. Traveling has changed from when I started as a young child, people aren't waiting to retire to hit the road. Social media has made it a popular and cool thing to do for millennials and working professionals nowadays. There are still the tried and true discount sites like Cheaptickets, Kayak, Orbitz, Expedia, TravelZoo and Priceline. And now Groupon has made it easier to track down great deals on airfare, hotel and car rental.

The smartphone takeover is the new age way of planning travel. You don't have to use a desktop to book a flight or plan travel. You can now do most of your travel planning on your phone. The technology is ever changing but all of it is making access to travel easier.

TRIP PLANNING: APPS

Tripnary. It's an app to assist mapping out your vacation based on your budget.

TripIt is a game changer, you can organize your travel plans via the app. When you get your flight itinerary (add car rental, hotel or restaurant reservations and activities if applicable) email: plans@tripit.com and it creates a daily detailed itinerary for you or if you have Gmail or Google Apps it creates one. Sync to your calendars, add or edit via the app or website.

Google Trips, Google Flights, Google Trip, all things travel for Google. This app is heavy on suggested things to do where you travel. It also offers food + drinks transportation options as well as things you should know. This is a great app with lots of information in one location.

Trip Case, a travel app that organizes and manages your trip. You can enter your itinerary manually or email Trip Case with the information. There is also an option to keep track of your expenses. It's an added feature for a fee.

BOOKING FLIGHTS:

Google Flights has your departure city saved, a map of possible destinations and prices for locations as soon as the site appears. Simply add your destination pick your flight from a list of results based on the lowest fares and your travel dates. It's better than the other discount travel sites, in my opinion. Only one tab opens up, it's clean and easy to navigate. I also use **SmartTravel Fare Alert** email deals that include places I've already searched so I can see the prices and snag a deal if the price drops. **Airfare Watch Dog** is another good one I like because of the social media factor. I see them post on Twitter all the time about deals from different destinations around the world. **Hopper** offers flight predictions so you know when to purchase a ticket for your trip. You can set it up to give you updates. This app is said to be great for frequent flyers. Try non US search engine sites like **Skycanner** and **Momondo** they will give you prices on smaller, budget and regional airlines that some sites might not otherwise. And of course, discount airlines like Jet Blue, SouthWest, Frontier, Alaska Airlines, Spirit Airlines are always offering deals. Sign up for their newsletters, to see the deals when they hit. I really like to fly Delta Airlines, my second choice is American Airlines so I receive their email alerts.

SLEEPING ARRANGEMENTS:

Staying in an acceptable hotel could make or break your trip. Despite the fact that you may not be in your hotel room much you still want to be comfortable. Checkout apps for lodging like **HotelTonight**, it's great for last minute deals on unsold rooms. **Airbnb**, offers unique rentals options from local host in cities across the world. **Design Hotels** and **Boutique Homes** are two more sites to check out, especially if you're in the market for luxury and designer hotels. **Booking.com** has an app version as well, unless you are familiar with the area in which you'd like to stay it can be hit or miss. I also recommend **Jetsetter** by TripAdvisor they offer hotels and last-minute travel deals via the website or app. If you get their newsletter, you'll see deals each day and some of the best travel articles out there. Become a member of clubs like Hilton Honors, SPG Starwood Hotels & Resorts, Marriott Rewards, Club Carlson Hotel Rewards Program and more is always a plus if you have a particular preference. Members receive special deals and benefits. Once you have accumulated a certain amount of points, they offer perks like a free night's stay. Ideally you want to lodge somewhere comfortable and reap the benefits as much as you possible can.

It doesn't matter how you book your travel just make sure you go somewhere. Make a commitment to visit one new

"After looking at the way things are on this earth, here's what I've decided is the best way to live: Take care of yourself, have a good time, and make the most of whatever job you have for as long as God gives you life. And that's about it. That's the human lot. Yes, we should make the most of what God gives, both the bounty and the capacity to enjoy it, accepting what's given and delighting in the work. It's God's gift! God deals out joy in the present, the now. It's useless to brood over how long we might have."

ECCLESIASTES 5:18-20 (MSG)

place each year and keep adding from there. The point is to broaden your horizon and enjoy the fruits of your labor.

- Take a course. Learn a craft. It's an opportunity to do something different after you've done what is needed of you. It is a perfect way to do you. Check a goal off your list. Do something for yourself that gives you joy.

- Pamper yourself. Briefly mentioned above, pampering is the best feeling especially anything in the form of relaxation. You deserve the time to let loose and chill. Spa days are the best way to pamper. It's a great way to connect with yourself and take a load off. I would also recommend going to the chiropractor, an alignment can do wonders to open up your body. Yoga is also good, it is a practice though and it's benefits are best on a consistent basis.

BONUS:
Try getting a monthly membership to a massage place like Massage Envy. The monthly membership is good for one service, a massage or facial. If you miss a month you just rack up services. If you're paying for it perhaps, you'll fit it into your schedule. SELF-care at its finest.

DAY 19
Questions

> Verse 28. "Her children arise and call her blessed; her husband also, and he praises her."

What information did you learn from this chapter?

_____

_____

_____

What is your take on bearing fruit?

_____

_____

_____

Why is it important to enjoy the fruits of your labor?

_____

_____

_____

_____

How can you enjoy your fruitfulness?

_____

_____

_____

Name the local spa's in your area. List the phone numbers and email addresses so they are readily available when you need them.

Name:

Phone:

Email:

Masseuse:

Name:

Phone:

Email:

Masseuse:

Name:

Phone:

Email:

Masseuse:

Make a list of things you like to do to relax. Try to incorporate at least one per week.

_____

_____

_____

Create a list of days and block of time you can free up for self-care time. The objective is to schedule the time to enjoy the fruits of your labor.

Monday:

Tuesday:

Wednesday:

Thursday:

Friday:

Saturday:

Sunday:

Books:

Everyday a Friday by Joel Osteen

The Road Less Traveled: A New Psychology of Love, Traditional Values, and Spiritual Growth by M. Scott Peck, M.D.

The Power of NOW: A Guide to Spiritual Enlightenment by Eckhart Tolle

The Art of Happiness by The Dalai Lama

The Gift of Imperfection by Brene Brown

Secrets of the Vine: Breaking Through to Abundance by Bruce Wilkinson

Bonus Comments:

_____

_____

_____

_____

_____

"Many women do noble things, but you surpass them all.

20

BE EXCELLENT

| Verse 29: "Many women do noble things, but you surpass them all."

Interpretation: Many of God's daughters have done virtuously but she surpassed them. Other women have had high moral standards, obtained wealth, power, "strength of character" but this woman, she is high above them. She is excellent, she was unmatched. She excels beyond everyone else. To *excel, is to be exceptionally good at or proficient in an activity or subject.* In this because she was really good at being a virtuous woman. She was better than the rest and it showed. I believe this spoke to her consistency and intent to do good. She shined, not only did her husband take notice but her children and the community, she was known throughout the gates.

| "The universe took it's time on you, crafted you precisely so you
| could offer the world something distinct from everyone else.
| So when you doubt how you were created you doubt an energy
| greater than us both."
| RUPI KAUR

APPLYING: BE EXCELLENT.

The slight difference between being good and excellent is like a gold medal versus a silver medal, one is better. There are good women, that

> "I find the best way to love someone is not to change them, but instead, help them reveal the greatest version of themselves."
>
> STEVE MARABOLI

is what we've been discussing this entire book. Having good morals, etc. What if you were not only good you were excellent? What's the difference? I believe excellence comes when you serve God. When you do things unto Him in excellence. When you "EXCELL" beyond what is good. To go above and beyond. Instead of Cum Laude you're Magna Cum Laude. You are at the top of your game. Not top of the income bracket but rather the way you conduct your life is in EXCELLence.

> "An excellent wife is the crown of her husband, but she who brings shame is like rottenness in his bones."
>
> PROVERBS 12:4 (ESV)

To be *excellent means to be extremely good, outstanding.* Extremely good, really good, like better than good. In this case be a woman with "Godfidence." Walk the path of God's truth, live a purpose filled life, have Godly thoughts that are proceeded with Godly action, strive to please God.

Now this doesn't mean that you look down on others. It simply means that you carry yourself in the highest regard. That you hold your head up high but also try to get others to see their greatness as well. That you accept people for who they are and where they are in life. You "excell" because you are confident in who you are and the God you serve. You have faith that can't be measured and walk with dignity and pride. You are in sync with your femininity and know that you are not to be compared to others because you are unique. You are distinguished because you are different, you are beyond good.

> "Spread love wherever you go. Let no one ever come to you without leaving happier."
> MOTHER TERESA

MAKE AN IMPACT: You have the ability to touch everyone you come in contact with. You can leave a positive impression or a negative one. The people you encounter will form some sort of opinion, not that it counts but wouldn't you rather leave an excellent one? I mean you are a P31 woman so your impact on others should always be on the up and up. Make people feel warm and welcomed. Try a simple smile, head gesture, even a hug. You don't have to be extra or uncomfortable but attempt to spread good energy and love. You never know how you can impact someone's life for the better.

LOVE. Your ability to give and receive love is preeminent. When you are in love with yourself it's super easy to give love away. Love is the foundation of being excellent in order to "excell." You know the power of love and have no problem displaying it freely. "And over all these virtues put on love, which binds them all together in perfect unity." Colossians 3:14 (NIV). I really like this verse from 1 Peter 4:8 (NIV), "Above all, love each other deeply, because love covers over a multitude of sins." Love is undeniably the best thing you can possess.

> "Darkness cannot drive out darkness; only light can do that. Hate cannot drive out hate; only love can do that."
> DR. MARTIN LUTHER KING, JR.

It is the love of God inside of you that shines through for all to see. The compassion you have for others is felt and reciprocated because its frequency is so high it cannot be denied. This is how you truly make an impact. You love like you've never been hurt, mistreated or hated. It erases what is opposite of love. Love is the answer, show more love.

> "Affection is when you see someone's strengths, love is when you accept someone's flaws."
> **UNKNOWN**

FAITH. All you have to have is a mustard seed and you have more than that. You trust God as your source and don't waiver when it comes to His faithfulness. Faith in the one that makes it all happen, you just have to have a little. To be excellent you may have to move mountains, you need faith for that. Faith to make the impossible possible. And all things are possible to them that believe. "Jesus looked at them and said, with man this is impossible, but with God all things are possible."

> "Don't dig up in doubt what you planted in faith."
> **ELIZABETH ELLIOT**

PRACTICE. I had a high school art teacher say, "Practice makes permanent." It's so true, practice doesn't make perfect as the saying goes, it does however make it permanent thus making it a habit. The awesome thing about practice is that it is not subject to one thing. You can practice on multiple things at one time. You can stop practicing something and totally focus on another thing. The possibilities are endless. Practice when others are asleep. "She sees that her trading is profitable, and her lamp does not go out at night." Proverbs 31:18 (NIV). But you must practice to become excellent.

EXCELLENCE. To have excellence at a particular thing takes practice and some development. You may have a knack for something and it is naturally easy for you. It will still require some practice to become really good in terms of excellence. Don't be afraid to form good habits to be great at something. It's all about consistency. Be efficient in your work, task, whatever you put your mind to. In this case be excellent at being a virtuous woman. "Excell" other women, be good. Stand out from the rest and not in a competitive way just in an "I'm awesome" way. Stand out in the crowd naturally and effortlessly.

> "We are what we repeatedly do. Excellence, then, is a habit."
> SOCRATES

UPLIFT. When you master a thing, it is up to you to teach someone else. The entire point of learning and perfecting something is to share it. Share it with friends and family, your community, the world. You can't be excellent and not give back. You can't keep the tools and information you learn all to yourself. Being excellent is not a selfish thing, it's all to get really good in order to help others. There is no way you were meant to be on this earth to be excellent and think no one else is capable of having excellence too. Again, it's not a competition it is becoming the very best version of yourself so that you can bring someone else along to do the same. Sharing is caring, uplifting one another is a form of servitude. Give of what you have perfected. And remember you can't beat God giving.

This woman was extraordinary and exquisite. The crème de la crème. She has that unspeakable, indescribable, je ne sais quoi type of presence. In all, she's a mystery. On the outside she does it with grace and efficiency. She is a great model to look up to.

EXCELLENT TIPS:

- Punctuality:
  This is good. Some say being on time is being late. Arrive a few minutes early to where you need to be.

- Respectful:
  Nothing better than being respectful and getting it right back. A P31 woman is always respectful, it is the classy and graceful way to go.

- Learn:
  Be willing to educate yourself. Continue to learn as much as you possibly can. It keeps your brain stimulated and you're never too old to learn something new.

- Responsible:
Be responsible not only with your time but your finances. Money management is vital in leaving a legacy for your family. It helps keep the house running properly.

- Simplicity:
The less things you have to concern yourself about the easier it is to get things done. Declutter your life and keep it simple.

- Flow:
I believe going with the flow is understanding that things won't always go your way and adjusting to change is good. It helps you deal with the situation, find the best solution and move forward. The quicker you move on the more productive you can be. Because your energy is focused on important things.

- Thankfulness:
Gratitude is truly the best attitude. You can't be excellent without having a heart of thankfulness. It should overflow in your life. It can really set you up for bountiful blessings. When you exude gratitude the energy you send out pumps the love in your heart. Love is the highest frequency so give more love and the really great and excellent things in life will come your way. To be excellent is to be thankful so make sure you have a thankful heart.

- Humility:
It's such a great characteristic. It is one that a P31 woman embodies. She thinks of herself highly but she's never too good to give and open her heart to others. She can sit on the throne and get in the trenches as well. She's never too proud, she is willing to do it for the cause and she won't boast or brag about the things she's done especially for others. She is in no need of a pat on the back, she's humble.

"Excellence is an art won by training and habituation. We do not act rightly because we have virtue or excellence, but we rather have those because we have acted rightly."

ARISTOTLE

DAY 20
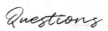

| Verse 29. "Many women do noble things, but you surpass them all."

What did you take from this chapter?

_____

_____

_____

What is your opinion on the difference between good and excellent?

_____

_____

_____

_____

Why is it important to "excell"?

_____

_____

_____

_____

How can you become excellent as a Proverbs 31 woman?

_____

_____

_____

_____

How can you show humility and "excell"?

_____

_____

_____

_____

Make a list of things you can do to become excellent?

_____

_____

_____

_____

Books:

The 7 Habits of Highly Effective People by Stephen R. Covey
Flow by Mihaly Csikszentmihalyi
Eat That Frog! 21 Great Ways to Stop Procrastinating by Brian Tracy
The Richest Man in Babylon by George S. Clason
Big Magic: Creative Living Beyond Fear by Elizabeth Gilbert

Bonus Comments:

_____

_____

_____

_____

_____

_____

_____

Charm is deceptive, and beauty is fleeting; **but a woman who** fears the Lord is to **be praised**.

21

HONOR GOD

> Verse 30: "Charm is deceptive, and beauty is fleeting; but a woman who fears the Lord is to be praised."

Interpretation: Charm is deceitful, body image and beauty are *vain, high or excessive opinion of one's self.* Beauty is fleeting, it's temporary. But fear the Lord and that will be praised.

As you age, you will change. Sin, worry, and stress age you and beauty is temporary. The value you put on looking good should not override your effort and commitment to God. I struggle with this. I love to work out and look good but I have to be mindful of my reasoning for doing so. There is a thin line between honoring the temple and working out for vanity's sake. I try to worship and honor God when I'm working out. Referencing Him with the music I listen to, thanking Him for the activity of my limbs, for keeping me healthy and injury-free sometimes I'll ask Him to help me push through a tough run. Overall, I hope He's pleased. I want to stay healthy to live longer, to be prepared for emergencies and to honor God by taking care of the temple, the house in which He trusted my spirit to live. I also watch what I eat, listen to and read because honoring God is referencing Him in all that I do, all that I invite into my temple.

Think of a temple in biblical days. People of different walks of life came to the temple. The greedy, mean, contentious, liars, gossipers, stone throwers, blasphemers, adulterers, fornicators, the sick and more came to the temple. The physical temple is a place of refuge to right the wrong, to turn evil to good, to make the crooked straight. A building made for worship to God, the house of God. The temple was a welcoming place for those who needed help. It was a gathering place to seek God.

The word temple can be used literally as well as figuratively. Take your body, your temple. It is the place in which your spirit dwells, it is a gathering place. You have to be mindful of what you let come into your temple. The descriptions above can enter into your temple, your space and energy if you are not careful. Spirits are lurking trying to see what you'll be responsive to. And if you leave so much as a window cracked or the door opened for too long, they will come in. All living things have spirits. You must also beware of what you eat. Remember there are different ways things can enter your body. So hearing, touching, speaking and sight should all be considered when talking about the temple. Watch what you subject yourself to, what "temple" you take your temple to and the people you surround yourself with. Remember that your body is sacred. Offer it to God as a living sacrifice. It's where your spirit lives, it is your connection to God.

My point is to beware of your temple, be careful as to what you invite and allow to be in your space. If it does not honor God then it should be removed. You must constantly check and make sure that you are in alignment with God and that what you do is honoring Him.

Excerpt from *Wild at Heart: Discovering the Secret of a Man's Soul* by John Eldredge:

"After years of hearing the heart-cry of women, I am convinced beyond a doubt of this: God wants to be loved. He wants to be a priority to someone. How could we have missed this? From cover to cover, from beginning to end, the cry of God's heart is, "Why won't you choose Me?" It is amazing to me how humble, how vulnerable God is on this point. "You will...find me," says the Lord, "when you seek me with all your heart" (Jer. 29:13). In other words, "Look for me, pursue me – I want you to pursue me." Amazing. As Tozer says, "God waits to be wanted."

APPLYING: HONOR GOD.

To honor God should always be the constant. Favor, it comes and goes. Outer beauty fades, the body changes over time but your reverence toward The Heavenly Father should not waiver. Favor and beauty are like that of sand, unstable and both have the ability to sink or change form. But to fear God is to build a foundation on solid rock. It is to place your life on a foundation of the promises of The Almighty. Any woman that lives a life on the foundation of the living God will be praised. Her life will at some point manifest that favor. And by honoring God she in turn will be honored.

> "Be my rock of refuge, to which I can always go; give the command to save me, for you are my rock and my fortress."
> **PSALM 71:3 (NIV)**

HOW TO HONOR GOD:

WHO. Honor God for who He is. They used to say, "If He doesn't do anything else, He's already done enough." It's true, just the life you have lived until this very page is priceless. The clothing, food, shelter and the extra bonuses in life like transportation are a huge blessing. But God is God. He is the best thing that could ever happen to you. And no matter what you decide to refer to Him as, the one true and living God is still on the throne. And for that He should be honored. He sees all, knows all and controls all. Honoring God is really simple when you think about it. To know God is to love God. There is peace when you know Him. Honor Him each day, live for Him, trust Him and love Him for who He is.

> "One of the most beautiful things that a woman can do is to walk in virtue; gracefully reflecting the purpose for which she was created, thus bringing glory to God."
> **DARLENE SCHACHT**

WALK. It takes a good amount of courage to walk with God. In a world of doing it your way it can be difficult to consider Him as a part of your daily life. It takes guts to go against the grain and stand firm in your beliefs. When the Romans are doing what the Romans do, you don't. You defy anything that is not like Him. You hold steadfast to His will for your life. Having the courage to live upright when it's popular to go in a different direction is admirable. God sees it and knows the struggle of today's distractions. The need and push to occupy your mind with illusions, images and unnecessary conflict. To have you so caught up in your career than you are in your purpose. He knows it is difficult to shine your light in darkness, He knows what you have to fight against on a daily basis, He knows your struggle. Honors those who honor Him, who live according to His will for their lives.

SACRIFICE. To honor God is to do unto God. To do unto God takes sacrifice. It is the ability to deny self and do for God. To allow His will for your life to prevail. To make a daily commitment to follow Him, to make Him a priority, let His light shine so that men may see Him in you. *Sacrifice, the act of giving up something valued for the sake of something else regarded as more important.* That is what it takes to have a relationship with God. In order to honor Him you have to make the sacrifice, letting go of your agenda and latching on to what God wants for your life. To deny what you want for what He wants. To say no to the flesh. To do away with what may seem natural and do what is spiritual. To live a life extraordinary through Him instead of ordinary doing what you think will work best for you. It is to include Him and not exclude Him. It is a sacrifice to go against the grain and deny your nature. When you choose to sacrifice it means that you are honoring God by regarding Him because it is more important than self. Make the sacrifice.

SURRENDER. I love the song "I Surrender All," it talks about surrendering all to God. Nothing left on your own, everything given to Him. Worry, doubt, fear, thoughts, circumstances, situations, dilemma's, decisions, people, relationships, finances, health, career, purpose, you name it. It is the release of all things. There is so much freedom in knowing that something greater than you has your best interest at heart. You are covered and protected by the one who controls all things. There is a peace that will overcome you to know that though life may bring on the good, bad and indifferent you are safe in the arms of the one that carries you. To surrender to the force that is greater than you is an excellent way to honor God. It is as simple as saying "God I surrender my all to you, I give you everything. Have your way in my life." Remember when you relinquish control you must trust Him completely.

TRUST. I personally believe this is one of the biggest attributes you can have when it comes to God and when it comes to relationships in general. You have to remember that a relationship with The Heavenly Father is to the liking of your most intimate relationships with humans. He wants more than anything to have an intimate relationship with you. Remember He is a jealous God. Just think of a jealous person, you know them when you see them. The constant need for attention and if it's not being given then there is a problem. It is no different with God. He's like "Hello, did I not wake you up this morning? You can at least say good morning or thanks. A simple acknowledgement of my grace for your life would be great." "How could you not see me in that, clearly nothing else would bless you like that. Hello. Come on dear child, you can't even give me a shoutout. Really? SMH." He is in continuous guard and careful watch over your life. He wants you to reference and honor Him for it.

Trusting God is being sure that He'll do what He said. To take His word as truth, to hold Him at His word, to believe and being patient as you wait on His promises to manifest. When it doesn't seem like things will pan out, trust Him. When things look less than stellar, trust Him. When life is crushing down on you, trust Him. When people turn their backs on you and reject you, trust Him. When everyone around you is being blessed and advancing but your time hasn't manifested yet, trust Him. When you feel like life is passing you by and you can't seem to find your way, trust Him. It takes practice to get to a place of complete trust. I believe it can be a bit difficult because you are trusting the invisible. But when you have a true intimate relationship with The Father it becomes normal to trust Him. He'll prove Himself to you over and over again. He'll prove His love and adoration to you daily. He will make your heart flutter with love.

Having patience is a key component when it comes to trust. It's huge because you have to have patience while you wait on God to do what He said He would do. You have to trust Him as you are practicing patience. The old saying, "He may not come when you want Him but He's right on time," applies here. You have to trust God as you wait patiently. To move on your own is a lack of trust. Taking over or trying to do something God can and will handle is not trusting Him to do it for you. Attempting to be God by taking over is not trust. Have the patience to wait on the Lord. "Wait on the Lord: be of good courage, and he shall strengthen thine heart: wait, I say, on the Lord." Psalms 27:14 (KJV). And as you patiently wait you automatically display trust. It's all a matter of trust.

> "Yours, Lord, is the greatness and the power and the glory and the majesty and the splendor, for everything in heaven and earth is yours. Yours, Lord, is the kingdom; you are exalted as head over all."
>
> **1 CHRONICLES 29:11 (NIV)**

THINGS YOU CAN DO TO HONOR GOD:

Keep Him first
Pray without ceasing
Trust Him
Honor Him
Respect + fear Him
Show gratitude
Keep a gratitude journal
Love others
Treat people with respect and dignity
Give to the needy
Serve others
Don't idolize people or things
Read the Bible
Study the Bible
Live by His commandments

> "Keep honoring God with your life, stay in peace, trust his timing and God will open doors that no man can shut."
>
> **JOEL OSTEEN**

DAY 21
Questions

> Verse 30. "Charm is deceptive, and beauty is fleeting; but a woman who fears the Lord is to be praised."

What did you learn from this chapter?

_____

_____

_____

What do you do to stay beautiful?

_____

_____

_____

_____

Does it take more time then you spend with God?

_____

_____

_____

_____

What does it mean to honor God?

_____

_____

_____

How do you honor Him on a daily basis?

_____

_____

_____

Make a list of ways you can incorporate God more each day:

_____

_____

_____

From the list above make a schedule that includes things from the list. Try scheduling alerts for prayer and devotion. What about honoring God by helping one person each day? Be intentional when you honor Him.

_____

_____

_____

_____

Books:
A Woman After God's Own Heart by Elizabeth George
Trusting God Day by Day: 365 Daily Devotions Joyce Meyer
Crazy Love: Overwhelmed by a Relentless God by Francis Chan

Bonus Comments:

_____

_____

_____

_____

_____

_____

_____

"

Honor her for all that her hands have done, **and let her works bring** her praise at **the city gate.**

"

22

WORK UNTO GOD

> Verse 31: "Honor her for all that her hands have done, and let her works bring her praise at the city gate."

Interpretation: Give her the fruit of her hands, let her own works praise her in the gates. Give her the product of her hands so she can enjoy her labor. Enjoying the fruits of her labor while she is still alive to experience it. She will be praised in the gates, not just by her family but by the entire town. The community watches her take care of her family and praises her.

Don't believe me just watch. It's about doing the work of God and letting it speak for itself. In this case she is praised. It's not forced she was just doing what she knew to do. There is honor in that and in this verse, we see the evidence of praise as a result.

APPLYING: WORK UNTO GOD.

This woman embodies God, her daily life is unto Him. She carries herself with dignity and grace. She puts God first above all else, this includes honoring her husband. Keep in mind that marriage is ministry, it is the most important ministry you'll be involved in, for your husband is your spiritual covering. It is a must to give attention to him because it also edifies God. It brings glory to God, it up builds His kingdom. That is what people see, they praise a woman and her efforts, for the fruits of her hands. What better fruit to bare than that of a husband and family? Building strong healthy families was always God's intent. When you focus on that it is pleasing in His sight and worthy of acknowledgement.

> "Therefore, my dear brothers and sisters, stand firm. Let nothing move you. Always give yourselves fully to the work of the Lord, because you know that your labor in the Lord is not in vain."
>
> 1 CORINTHIANS 15:58 (NIV)

Keep in mind that you will only be used at the level of your submission. You can't possible think that God will use you at full capacity if you're only giving Him half. It's like any other relationship, for the most part you get what you put into it. The Heavenly Father is no different. He is a jealous God. So full submission to His will yield great results. He is faithful to do what He said He is not a man that He should lie, He is truly a promise keeper. You just have to have full trust and faith that He will come through. Then do the work.

Excerpt from *Wild at Heart: Discovering the Secret of a Man's Soul* by John Eldredge:

"A woman of true beauty is a woman who in the depths of her soul is at rest, trusting God because she has come to know him to be worthy of her trust. She exudes a sense of calm, a sense of rest, and invites those around her to rest as well. She speaks comfort; she knows that we live in a world at war, that we have a vicious enemy, and our journey is through a broken world. But she also knows that because of God all is well, that all will be well. A woman of true beauty offers others the grace to be and the room to become. In her presence, we can release the tension and pressure that so often grips our hearts. We can breathe in the truth that God loves us and he is good."

CULTIVATE. Create ways in your daily life to work for Him. If you have a full-time career you have to cultivate ways to make sure that you spend quality time. Figure out when you can best do things to advance the kingdom. Often times this will be a matter of being in a constant state of awareness and just letting your light shine. Be loving and kind. Help others, especially when it is not convenient. Talk about His goodness when the opportunity presents itself, say encouraging words to someone in need, remain positive despite what things may look like spread love and pray for others. In order to cultivate God in your life you have to go into the day being intentional about letting your light shine. Consistently exude His love, in turn it will overflow and spill onto others.

> "Give unto the Lord the glory due unto his name; worship the Lord in the beauty of his holiness."
>
> **PSALM 29:2 (KJV)**

WORSHIP. There isn't anything He wants more than your worship. And you can worship Him by merely living your life. By modeling His son and keeping His commandments. *Worship, is the feeling or expression of reverence and adoration for a deity. Praise, express warm approval or admiration.* So, praise is an expression as well. Worship is specific to a deity or a god, in this case I am only talking about the true and living God. You can praise anyone but worship is specific adoration for God.

I will sometimes turn on some gospel music and exercise. I dedicate my workouts to Him, I'm so grateful to have the activity of my limbs. I worship and praise and that is what you can do all day. You can do things in your daily life to worship Him. To show adoration in your own way. It's really that simple. Constant gratitude is great too, it's the acknowledgement of something God has done for you, or thanking Him in advance for what you are believing Him to do. Gratitude is the best attitude. A simple thank you can go a long way.

I think if you think of God as a person, it makes it easier. "What would Jesus do?" I think it should be, "How would God feel?" It's just a good way to consider Him before you do things. Walking with Him daily and making sure to include Him. Living your life for Him is a form of worship.

HONOR. To *honor* is to show high respect or esteem. The work isn't really work if you know what I mean, it's a lifestyle, a spiritual quest, a journey with God. It's unlike any other relationship you will ever have. And the honor and respect become automatic when your life is all about God. You reference Him in all you do. Esteem Him so high, respect like you would an elder, grandparent, mentor, pastor, spiritual confidant. Remember not to ever reference man more than God. It is honorable to honor God. He loves it as well as He loves you.

> "The soul of the sluggardly desireth, and hath nothing: but the soul of the diligent shall be made fat."
> **PROVERBS 13:4 (KJV)**

LIVE. Do as unto the Lord. Live your life for God. Working to please Him and only Him. Honor the power of His might. Referencing and honoring His will for your life, experience life with like-minded people, cultivate deep connections and fellowship with them. Create communities that will ultimately help all of humanity by merely living. Allow your spiritual practice to be a part of each day. This is how you work unto God, just live.

God wants you to be happy. I believe that is the reason He made us in His image. To enjoy all that He has created. He gave us the ability to make choices. That is how awesome He is. He wants us to choose Him. He wants us to live for Him. Each day, He wants us to commune with Him. To talk, walk and bask in His presence. To work unto God is a privilege and an honor. To be chosen to follow Him is a badge of honor and all He wants is the favor of your dedication to living a life for Him.

Now I do believe that living and working unto to God also has to do with hard work in general. Being lazy and working for God do not go hand in hand. He is not pleased with those who do not work hard.

> "Go to the ant, you sluggard; consider its ways and be wise! It has no commander, no overseer or ruler, yet it stores its provisions in summer and gathers it's food at harvest. How long will you lie there, you sluggard? When will you get up from your sleep? A little sleep, a little slumber, a little folding of the hands to rest- and poverty will come on you like a thief and scarcity like an armed man."
> **PROVERBS 6:6-11 (NIV).**

He intended for us to be self-efficient like the ant. You don't need someone to look over your shoulder telling you what to do. You definitely know what to do. And if you are an entrepreneur and following your passion, you're creating your own path. You know what is required for you to see results. God will bless you when you're working unto Him.

You can't help but be successful and prosper because you work for God. Utilize the gifts that He has given you.

Don't hesitate to reach out to mentors, advisers, wise counsel to help guide you along the way. Use your resources. God gave you the necessary tools, tap into them and by all means, for the love of God make them work for you.

LOVE. I have talked about love a lot in this book. Self-love, loving others and now to the love of God. To know God is to love God. To be in close relationship with Him is like having the upmost respect and gratitude for a parent that will do anything for you. The unconditional love a parent shows you pales in comparison to the love The Creator has for you. Nothing else can ever measure up. There is no one that will come into your life that knows you better than Him. There isn't anyone that can do for you the way His does. NO ONE. Nothing else matters more than His creation to love Him back the way He loves us.

It is not only your love for The Father it's your love for humankind. When you have the love of God on the inside you can't help but love others. God's love teaches you to love yourself. And by loving yourself and understanding why God created you you have no room for hate, malice or behavior that is less than stellar. Love for self and the love of God shines through. You don't even have to say a word most of the time, your presence says it all. The love and joy just come through like rays of sunshine. It shines so bright that those that come in contact with you need sunglasses. You attract all types of people because they want to be close to the light. The light is the love. Love God, love yourself, love others.

"Blessed is the man that walketh not in the counsel of the ungodly, nor standeth in the way of sinners, nor sitteth in the seat of the scornful. But his delight is in the law of the Lord; and in his law doth he meditate day and night. And he shall be like a tree planted by the rivers of water, that bringeth forth his fruit in his season; his leaf also shall not wither; and whatsoever he doeth shall prosper."

PSALM 1:1-3 (KJV)

WORK WAYS:

Walk with God
Talk with God
Incorporate God in your daily life
Keep praying
Ask God what you should do
Keep the faith
Don't be lazy, model the ant
Read and study the Bible
Worship Him
Cultivate a lifestyle that keeps Him in Mind
Let His will be done
Love Him with your whole heart
Have a heart of servitude
Exercise your desire to give
Be open to His will for your life
Say yes to His will
Follow His instructions
Listen intently to His voice
Turn from your own sinful ways
Tell others about God
Let your light shine

I don't know about you but some days can just go away. It's like "end already and let's start completely over tomorrow." I'm sure you can relate. And when it seems like I've had a series of bad days I scream and cry out to God, "Like WTH?!" I kid you not. We're on that level. It's a relationship and in any relationship, there are going to be questions and frustrating times. If I didn't have questions and knew all of the answers then why would I need God? Exactly. I need Him and when I have a question I ask. When I'm frustrated, I talk like I'm frustrated, I don't have the patience to go through the semantics. He gets me. I'm like Peter maybe David sometimes with my expressions. My heart is in the right place and by merely reaching out is referencing God. It's including Him in my life and that is relationship.

God wants a relationship with YOU. It took me, a Pastor's kid decades to figure it out. The most important thing is the connection you have with God. The ways in which you honor Him are countless, some of which I mentioned in this book. Remember God is a jealous God. You must not get tied up in the tangible things of this world. What is most important is what you cannot see. The soul of an individual, oxygen, your bodily functions, God Himself. The invisible is powerful. It is powerful because the connection is to God, the maker of all. The Creator of all there is and will ever be. The source. All roads lead to Him. If you don't learn anything else from this book please know this, God loves you and He wants to have a loving relationship with you. Get to know Him, honor Him, work unto Him.

PRAYER. You can't really work unto Him if you don't pray. Like how is that going to really work? I'm talking to myself too. You can't say that you walk with God and not pray and pray all the time. I know some women who can just have a conversation like God himself is right there listening and talking back. Women who speak with the most profound vocabulary, it can be rather intimidating. Even when the pastor or others go before people and pray it's like they all took a class on how to pray. Saying the right words in the right tone and is just, wow. And then you get home in your quite place and try and it's just not the same. Ha! Praying is really talking to God. You want to reference and honor Him so praising Him is good to do starting off, show your gratitude, talk to Him. Refrain from a bunch of personal requests, He knows what you need. Most of the time should be spent in a state of gratitude then praying for others.

Make sure you give Him time to answer or respond back to you. This may be hard. The deeper relationship the easier it gets. Sit still and silent, wait for Him to speak to you. It may not be about what you prayed; it could be something else. He may instruct you to do something. He hears all so don't worry. Whatever it may be, is between you and Him. Be sure not to have a one-sided conversation, you talking the entire time. It's like the girlfriend that talks and talks about what's going on with her and you listen and you're not given a chance to respond. By the time it comes around to you she has to get off, not cool. And that's what God is like with us, the girlfriend that just listens and can't talk so let Him speak.

> "When you pray be sure that you listen as well as talk. You have things to say to God but He also has things He wants to say to you."
>
> **JOYCE MEYER**

I think writing prayers are good for times when you don't know what to say verbally. You can read them when you don't have enough to say or don't know where to start. Try creating prayers of your own. Type them out, write them down on something you can get to when you need it. Use the prayer examples I have provided. I love the Lord's Prayer when I'm at a loss. I also find when I'm feeling anxiety about the basic things in life that is a perfect time to quote God's word until I feel better. I say "God shall supply ALL my needs according to His riches in glory," whenever I feel worry trying to creep up. God doesn't make promises He won't keep. His word is true. His word is the same yesterday, today and forevermore. My prayer is that you use these prayers when you need them. That you share them with those who desire to start a prayer life. And that God will be the moving force in your life.

Start off with praise and gratitude

Pray for others

Personal request (he knows your needs, if you have request be specific)

Gratitude

Stillness or silence to listen

Close

DAILY PRAYER

Dear Heavenly Father,

I love you.
You are the air I breathe, the oxygen that allows me to stay alive.
Thank you so much for this day.
Thank you for another opportunity to be in your presence.
Today I dedicate to you. I surrender my will to yours.
I answer the call of your voice and command.
I honor you with all that I am.
Help me to walk and talk with you.
To be an example to those who do not know you and those who need you.
Give me the strength and fortitude to push through challenges of any kind.
Keep me from hurt, harm or danger.
Give me peace that cannot be comprehended.
Turn my darkness into light.
Be my guide.
You are necessary.
I need you.
I welcome you today.
With all that I have and all that I am...
Thank you

FAITH PRAYER

Dear Heavenly Father,

I am in awe of you.
I know that you can do more than I can ever ask for or think.
I expect great things because I live a life that is pleasing to you.
I know that you are capable of doing it again.
I know that your perfect love will rid me of any fear.
There is no reason to doubt the promises you have for my life.
I have a mustard seed of faith, that is all that is required of me.
I trust you, therefore my faith will not waiver.
I am calm and at peace knowing that you hold my hand.
I have total confidence in you.
I will not worry
I will not fret
You are working things out for my good.
I turn everything over to you
I have faith
I have faith in you...
Thank you

PRAISE PRAYER

Dear Heavenly Father,

You are an awesome God
How amazing are your works?
Very detail to perfection. Each function designed immaculately
I was made in your image and there are no mistakes
My life is an extension of your love
I have purpose. I was created for your purpose
My love extends to you
When I feel low you lift me up
You send the sunshine on a cloudy day
Your beauty I see in the vast land you created
Knowing you is heaven on earth
You are better to me than I am to myself
The best thing that has ever happened to me
You are all I'll ever need
Thank you for creating me
Thank you for your love
Thank you for all that you do,
even when I don't recognize it
Thank you for always supplying my needs
Thank you for choosing me
I praise you
I worship you...
Thank you

SURRENDER PRAYER

Dear Heavenly Father,

I surrender my all to you God
There is none like you
You are the God of all Gods
The King of all Kings
You are the master of my soul
The Creator of all that is
I give back to you what you have given to me, my life
My life is yours to do what you want
I am a living sacrifice
I turn over everything to you
I leave nothing of my own
No worry, doubt or fear
Change my mind, allow my thoughts to be your thoughts
Every circumstance, situation, dilemma I give to you
I release my relationships with people
My finances, health, career and purpose
I release all things
I surrender all
I rest safely in your arms, the safest place I know
I love you
I desperately need you
I'm surrendering...
Thank you

Wow, I felt the power of that prayer as I wrote. God is real. I pray you release all you have to Him. Let the mighty one handle it. All He wants you to do is cast your cares upon Him. When your heart is heavy, give it to Him. When all hope is lost, give it to Him. If people turn their backs on you, give it to Him. For He truly cares about you no matter where you are in life. Surrender.

> "In the same way, let your light shine before others, that they may see your good deeds and glorify your Father in heaven."
> **MATTHEW 5:16 (NIV)**

DAY 22
Questions

> Verse 31. "Honor her for all that her hands have done, and let her works bring her praise at the city gate."

What did you take away from this chapter?

_____

_____

_____

How would you describe your relationship with God?

_____

_____

_____

How can you improve it?

_____

_____

_____

_____

Serving others is a way to work unto God. Make a list of other ways you can work unto God:

_____

_____

_____

Praying is important. Based on the sample prayers in the book create your own below. Write a daily prayer or create one more specific like protection, family, finances, purpose, etc. Then use it.

_____

_____

_____

Books:
The Power of Simple Prayer by Joyce Meyer
Finding I Am by Lysa TerKeurst
Draw the Circle: The 40 Day Prayer Challenge by Mark Batterson
Get Your Life Back by John Eldredge
Jesus Always by Sarah Young

Bonus Comments:

_____

_____

_____

_____

23

DON'T BE THIS WOMAN

Let's be frank. You look at someone else's life and you say, "Wow, I know I have my ways but I'm not THAT bad." Or something similar. Admit it, I'm guilty for sure. It makes you feel better about yourself. In reality it really is being judgmental, and you don't want to be that lady. Stay in the judge free zone, life is better that way. Looking in the mirror and examining yourself is always best. When you are too busy mastering self you don't have time or energy to judge anyone else.

In mastering self, there are some things to avoid. Perhaps you have to stop doing a thing. Life is about learning and growing. It is a series of courses that God presents and that course is as long as it needs to be until you pass the test to move to the next course. All courses combined equate to your overall journey or life. The more you evolve and become one with whom God created you to be the more impact you have on others. There is a reason you are here, a purpose to live out. As you evolve you get better and better. And that has every bit to do with this bonus chapter of sorts. When you know, you do better. This entire book is really that, doing better. Cultivating a standard of goodness. Getting it right and setting the tone for others to model.

I was doing research on this topic of being a noble and virtuous woman and I came across some scriptures that were not so good. Eve's spirit runs rapid even today. Lack of accountability, easily deceived, manipulation, eye catching weakness (just like men, women like what is pleasing to the eye), control, trust deficiency with God. These are attributes that Eve possessed. She also made a major decision without talking to Adam, her covering and protection. This life altering decision changed everything. It showed her lack of submission to Adam as well. They passed down sin nature. As mentioned in chapter 3 "Be Good" the pecking order was established after the fall, after sin. It is human nature to walk beside your husband. Because of the curse and punishment for sinning woman is to submit to man. It's not a bad thing ladies. You can still walk in purpose and be submissive to your husband. That command is for your husband only. In a marriage where the husband is totally connected to God it is easy to submit. And by submitting you are honoring God.

Excerpt from my Women Series, a series of short stories: To submit…

"Genesis 3:16, "Unto the woman he said, I will greatly multiply the sorrow and thy conception; in sorrow thou shalt bring forth children; and thy desire shall be to thy husband, and he shall rule over thee." The fall and the curse have everything to do with the dynamic of humankind. Sin or evil vs good or righteous and obedience. The woman committed wrong, took no accountability for her actions, convinced man to take part in the wrong and both were cursed as a result. We are still living under that curse. So, when punishments were handed out The Creator had to go against His design for both woman and man, to walk together.

"On the subject of women specifically it's says "I will greatly multiply thy sorrow," it's the feeling of deep distress caused by loss or disappointment or misfortune suffered by oneself or others. This can probably equate to women's emotions. By nature, women are nurtures but take that and add sorrow, greatly multiply the sorrow. God's design for women to nurture, which means to care for and encourage the growth or development of. To be a help-meet, to provide what man lacks. To be the feminine extension of God. The opposite of man. Like the sun and moon, light and darkness, hot and cold, are male and female. God also designed woman to be giver of life, a beauty, alluring in her mind, soul and physicality. She is mesmerizing and The Creator's most beautiful masterpiece. The envy of the enemy.

"You don't think that the enemy was jealous of someone more beautiful than him? He sought to destroy her. The attack of a woman's beauty is a trick of the enemy. You break her down, it's the downfall of humankind of mother earth…the giver of life. He did that with deception. And the curse is being lived out even today. God's intention was for man and woman to co-exist, to co-manage, to rule as one. The curse made woman subject to man. "Man shall rule over woman." It is against woman's nature, her walk was to be beside her man. That's your struggle, your nature."

Eve, our first example of a wife. Boy did she miss the mark. God truly showed her mercy but not without a cost. And that is still true for God. He will show us mercy but sin, cost. The wages of sin is death. Each time we sin it kills us spiritually and could draw us closer to a physical death. It disconnects us from The Father. If you cannot submit to The Father totally then you are going to have an extremely hard time submitting to your husband. Remember when you know better you do better, right? So, ladies let's try not to be this wife. You can be a GOOD wife instead. Thanks to my Dad for help on the chapter.

DON'T BE THIS WOMAN:

FOOLISH:

> "The foolish woman is dulled to wisdom, calloused to correction and sluggish in her response to God."
> RAYMOND E. LLOYD JR.

Proverbs 9:13-18 (KJV) "A foolish woman is *clamorous* (loud) she is simple, and knoweth nothing. For she sitteth at the door of her house, on a seat in the high places of the city, To call passengers who go right on their ways: Whoso is simple, let him turn in hither: and as for him that wanteth understanding, she says to him, Stolen waters are sweet, and bread eaten in secret is pleasant. But he knoweth not that the dead are there; and that her guests are in the depths of hell."

Proverbs 14:1 (NIV) "The wise woman builds her house, but with her own hands the foolish one tears hers down." *Foolish* in Hebrew means *dull, thick, sluggish. Tears down* meaning *to overthrow, to destroy* in Hebrew. Conversation by conversation, circumstance by circumstance, relationship by relationship, brick by brick she dismantles her house. She troubles her house so long with her own hands and will only inherit the wind, nothing tangible. "He who brings ruin on his family will inherit only wind, and the fool will be servant to the wise." Proverbs 11:29 (NIV)

Proverbs 14:8 (KJV) "The wisdom of the prudent is to understand this way; but the folly of fools is deceit."

Proverbs 19:13 (NIV) "A foolish child is a father's ruin, and a quarrelsome wife is like a constant dipping of a leaky roof."

It does not pay to be a fool. It is far from being Godly and far from being a P31 woman. Wisdom, knowledge and understanding are vital to success, following God and living a good life.

CONTENTIOUS:

Contentious is defined in Hebrew as *one given to strife, one easily angered, a nag, one who is argumentative.* She can't be stopped and is man's misery.

Proverbs 20:3 (NLT) "Avoiding a fight is a mark of honor; only fools insist on quarreling." *Quarrel* in Hebrew means *to burst forth in a rage, a tantrum.*

Proverbs 21:9 (NIV) "Better to live on a corner of the roof than share a house with a quarrelsome wife."

Proverbs 21:19 (NIV) "Better to live in a desert than with a quarrelsome and nagging wife."

Proverbs 27:15-16 (NLT) "A quarrelsome wife is as annoying as constant dripping on a rainy day. Stopping her complaints is like trying to stop the wind or trying to hold something with greased hands."

You have witnessed this woman at some point in your life. If you have seen this in public only imagine what it is like in the home of a contentious woman. She is contending, fighting all the time. Nothing is ever right or to her liking. The root of that is the lack of love, self-love. At some point something happened and there was no love, her love was abused, she never knew her self-worth. She never took the time to love herself and seek God for validation.

You may be her. I say to you let God love you. There is no greater love, no greater love. Spend time with Him, getting to really know Him. I promise He'll turn your life around. The only thing you need to contend and fight against is the enemy. And you'll learn to do that with the spirit. My heart goes out to you. Be happy. God will show you happiness and freedom. He'll give you a peace that you cannot comprehend. You don't have to be this woman. God is showing you how to be good and walk in goodness. READ CHAPTER ONE AGAIN.

INDISCREET:

> "The indiscreet woman is the shallow woman. She lacks depth and insight. The indiscreet woman lacks common sense but she is beautiful. And so to cover up for her lack of common sense and perception she works on her beauty. A person that lacks discretion is one who is imperceptive, unaware, gullible, without reality, and at times naïve."
> RAYMOND E. LLOYD JR.

Ecclesiastes 7:26 (NIV) "I find more bitter than death the woman who is a snare, whose heart is a trap and whose hands are chains. The man who pleases God will escape her, but the sinner she will ensnare."

Proverbs 11:22 (NIV) "Like a gold ring in a pig's snout is a beautiful woman who shows no discretion." In Hebrew *discretion* means *taste*. The difference in having taste and being tasteless, lacking the knowledge of right and wrong and what is appropriate and inappropriate. As well as the lack of overall character, it mocks her beauty.

> "A woman lacking discretion no matter how beautiful becomes as repulsive as the runny nose of a pig. And her physical beauty, like the gold ring, seems totally out of place."
> RAYMOND E. LLOYD JR.

She has it so she flaunts it, it is all she thinks she has to offer. Her beauty is only skin deep. She is a luxury car on the outside with cheap parts on the inside. She lacks depth and strengthening her mind and spirit is the last thing she'd spend her time doing. She would rather focus on the exterior. She lacks class and grace. She is beautifully out of place like a gold ring in a pig's nose. She too lacks self-love. And the love of God she does not know.

SENSUOUS:

> "Right and wrong are not important to her; only what is sweet and pleasant. Her focus on a live-for-the-moment lifestyle is short-sighted and blurs her eyes to the long-term effects of her actions thus validating that she is truly naïve, and knows nothing. She can look you eyeball to eyeball and without batting a lash, deceive you in the most convincing way."
>
> **RAYMOND E. LLOYD JR.**

Proverbs 2:16-19 (KJV) "To deliver thee from the strange woman, even from the stranger which flattereth with her words; Which forsaketh the guide of her youth, and forgetteth the covenant of her God. For her house inclineth unto death, and her paths unto the dead. None that go unto her return again, neither take they hold of the paths of life." *Strange*, meaning *estranged, alienated*. She is far from how she was raised, away from those who taught her right from wrong. She is distant from the God that is always there.

Proverbs 5:3-6 (NIV) "For the lips of an adulteress woman drip honey, and her speech is smoother than oil; but in the end she is bitter as gall, sharp as a two-edged sword. Her feet go down to death; her steps lead straight to the grave. She gives no thought to the way of life; her paths wander aimlessly, but she does not know it."

Proverbs 6:23-26 (KJV) "For the commandment is a lamp; and the law is light; and reproofs of instruction are the way of life: To keep thee from the evil woman, from the flattery of the tongue of a strange woman. Lust not after her beauty in thine heart; neither let her take thee with her eyelids. For by means of a whorish woman a man is brought to a piece of bread; and the adulteress will hunt for the precious life."

Proverbs 7:5-12 (NIV) "They will keep you from the adulteress woman, from the wayward woman with her seductive words. At the window of my house I looked down through the lattice. I saw among the simple, I noticed among the young men, a youth who had no sense. He was going down the street near her corner, walking along in the direction of her house at twilight, as the day was fading, as the dark of night set in. Then out came a woman to meet him, dressed like a prostitute and with crafty intent. She is unruly and defiant, her feet never stay at home; now in the street, now in the squares, at every corner she lurks."

Proverbs 7:25-27 (NIV) "Do not let your heart turn to her ways or stray into her paths. Many are the victims she has brought down; her slain are a mighty throng. Her house is a highway to the grave, leading down to the chambers of death."

You can turn your life around with the decision to do better. If you realize there are some areas in your life that need improvement start today. Don't delay making small changes to become a better person. It takes time, prayer, effort and lots of patience but you can do it. It's so much better being good than having characteristics like the woman in this chapter. Most importantly, God sees it and He honors it. I know you can do it.

BONUS CHAPTER
Don't Be This Woman.

What did you learn from this chapter?

_____

_____

_____

_____

Make a list of scriptures that stood out:

_____

_____

_____

_____

Can you identify with any of the characteristics of the woman described?

_____

_____

_____

_____

What do you think you can do to improve?

_____

_____

_____

_____

Books:
Woman thou art Healed & Whole by T.D. Jakes
Woman Thou Art Loosed by T.D. Jakes
Captivating by John & Stasi Eldredge

Bonus Comments:

_____

_____

_____

_____

_____

_____

_____

_____

P31 APPLICATION BREAKDOWN BY VERSE

10: KNOW YOUR WORTH.

11: BE FEMININE.

12: BE GOOD.

13: BE RESOURCEFUL.

14: ANTICIPATE HIS NEEDS.

15: SET THE TONE.

16: KNOW WHAT'S GOING ON.

17: STAY ACTIVE.

18: BE ACCESSIBLE.

19: DO THE WORK OR HIRE SOMEONE.

20: GIVE TO THOSE IN NEED.

21: BE PREPARED.

22: BE A QUEEN.

23: ADVANCE YOUR HUSBAND.

24: OWN YOUR OWN BUSINESS.

25: BE CONFIDENT.

26: SPEAK WISELY.

27: STAY BUSY + ALERT.

28: ENJOY YOUR FRUITFULNESS.

29: BE EXCELLENT.

30: HONOR GOD.

31: WORK UNTO GOD.

Final THOUGHTS

Honestly this was just me preparing myself for marriage with no intention to write a book. But God would have it otherwise and I totally trust His plan and perfect will for my life. So, I did my work, for now at least, and if He adds something else I'll do that too. I am open to what I am supposed to do for Him. One day in the near future I will be presented to the man God has for me. In the meantime, I wait. I work and produce fruit.

I trust God's perfect will for my life and I implore you to do the same. It allows you to do the light work and God to handle the real work. I mean, He does it so well, why do we constantly try to interfere with the Master? I believe the phrase "Get out of your own way," is really like saying get out of God's way, let Him lead. Move over, step aside and clear the path so that He can take control. That is major for Him. Let there be no gods above Him. Take a look at what you do in your life that trumps God. Be mindful that He is to be number one in your life. And in making your husband your number one earthly responsibility, you are honoring God in the process. The three of you (God, hubby, YOU) are uniting for the upbuilding of the Kingdom. And that's good, really good.

I know that this noble, virtuous woman is pretty much like a unicorn. But with help and modern advancements in technology, this chick is an ideal model for a good woman. I believe with focus and the proper time management, she can be duplicated and surpassed. I pray you were able to grasp the concepts and use the resources provided. I pray if you are single and desire to be married, that God presents you when the time is right. I pray if you are married, with or without children, that you can become a better wife and mother for your family. All in all, I pray this is the RISE OF THE GOOD WOMAN.

"**Let us not become weary** in doing good, **for at the proper time we will** reap a harvest **if we do not** give up."

Galatians 6:9 (NIV)

Special
ACKNOWLEDGMENTS

Here's to women all over the world trying to find their way. Who are striving to be and do better in this world. Who understand the importance of sharing and forging sisterhoods. Who hold it down for their families and communities. Women who show love and great energy. You are beautiful. You rock.

Special thanks to my parents, siblings, family and friends. My blog subscribers, Facebook friends, Twitter and Instagram followers. Those who have ever encouraged, prayed, extended a helping hand to me, thank you. Special appreciation to Ernie Suggs for your editing expertise. Thank you to the friends who extended their time to read and critique chapters.

Huge thank you to my best friend Barbara Copeland who let me lock myself in her house to write this book. My accountability partner for cheering me on and keeping me in line. My mentor for seeing the vision and encouraging me throughout the years. Thanks to the staff at Mynd Matters Publishing for partnering me on this journey.

Extra special thanks to my sister Robin, you inspire me daily. Thanks for your love and support. To my mothers, who I was able to draw from to help write this book, I love you both. To my father, Raymond E. Lloyd Jr., I appreciate you more than you'll ever understand. Thanks for letting me use your research and teaching me that no matter what life throws at me, I'll land on my feet and continue to thrive.

Thank you, God, for words from mind to paper, your unconditional love, grace and mercy. Thank you for choosing me.

"The true meaning of life is to plant trees, under whose shade you do not expect to sit."

-Nelson Henderson

ABOUT THE AUTHOR

Stacy Lloyd is the owner of ms lloyd enterprises, Ltd Co., a multi-media + marketing firm. A family venture she runs with her sisters. Her responsibilities include the planning, development and implementation of all projects from talent services to artwork. That would include Proverbs 31 instructional videos, DIY projects, merchandising and branding for all things ms lloyd enterprises.

Ms Lloyd has a broadcast journalism background spanning more than 20 years. Working in both local news and entertainment news sectors. She has experience producing, radio news reporting, hosting and acting.

She is enthusiastic about travel and the love of people, she writes inspirational blogs to encourage individuals to live their best lives. In an ideal world she would travel the globe, write and inspire others.

Stacy is an Ohio native and now calls Atlanta home. She is currently working on publishing others books, implementing the vision of ms lloyd enterprises and other platforms to help people become their best self.

STAY CONNECTED

Instagram & Twitter: @risegoodwoman

www.msstacylloyd.com
Instagram: @msstacylloyd
Facebook: MsStacy Lloyd
Twitter: @msstacylloyd

Love Ya!

American Red Cross Emergency Contact Card

Get a kit. Make a plan. Be informed.

Directions:
* Print out a card for every member of your household.
* Fill in your emergency contact information.
* Carry this card with you to reference in the event of a disaster or other emergency.

Important Phone Nos.

Police: Call 9-1-1 or _____
Fire Dept.: Call 9-1-1 or _____
Ambulance: Call 9-1-1 or _____
Poison Control Center: 800-222-1222
Health Care Provider: _____

Emergency Contact Card

Name: _____

Phone: _____

Home Address: _____

People to Call or Text in an Emergency

_____
_____
_____
_____
_____
_____

_____
_____
_____
_____
_____

Out-of-Area Contact Person: _____
Phone: _____

Meeting Place Outside of Neighborhood: _____

Important Phone Nos.

Police: Call 9-1-1 or _____
Fire Dept.: Call 9-1-1 or _____
Ambulance: Call 9-1-1 or _____
Poison Control Center: 800-222-1222
Health Care Provider: _____

Emergency Contact Card

Name: _____

Phone: _____

Home Address: _____

People to Call or Text in an Emergency

_____
_____
_____
_____
_____
_____

_____
_____
_____
_____
_____

Out-of-Area Contact Person: _____
Phone: _____

Meeting Place Outside of Neighborhood: _____

Fold Here

Fold Here

Fold Here

CPSIA information can be obtained
at www.ICGtesting.com
Printed in the USA
BVHW030223120421
604721BV00020B/98